CAREER MANAGEMENT

Other books by **Marion S. Kellogg**

What to Do About Performance Appraisal (AMA, 1965)
Closing the Performance Gap (AMA, 1967)
Putting Management Theories to Work (Gulf Publishing Company, 1968)
When Man and Manager Talk (Gulf Publishing Company, 1969)

CAREER MANAGEMENT

Marion S. Kellogg

American Management Association, Inc.

HF 11314
5549
.P7
K29

© American Management Association, Inc., 1972.
All rights reserved. Printed in the United States of
America.

This publication may not be reproduced, stored in a
retrieval system, or transmitted in whole or in part,
in any form or by any means, electronic, mechanical,
photocopying, recording, or otherwise, without the
prior written permission of the Association.

International standard book number: 0-8144-5226-4
Library of Congress catalog card number: 73-173319

First printing

Foreword

This book is written for progressive business executives and their hard-working personnel directors. It outlines an opportunity to add to the quality of the working life of professional and management employees by focusing attention on career advancement systems for them. It recommends improvements in current systems and offers specific suggestions for opening the promotion process to joint employee-management decision making.

In one sense, it is based on experience. Over the years, I've talked to large numbers of employees in many different kinds of organizations. They've described their feelings and desires and related tales of how the promotion systems of their companies actually work. I've talked to managers who have freely expressed their concern about their part in helping or impeding the careers of associates. I've talked to personnel people who have described their struggle to devise better ways of finding qualified candidates for higher-level positions. I have personally been in all three roles—employee, manager, and personnel specialist. The unidentified quotes throughout this book reflect comments made directly to me, and I have built my recommendations on these contributions as well as on my personal experience.

FOREWORD

On the other hand, I have not seen a complete system such as I describe in operation in any one place. One module exists in one company and one in another; some segments function in government institutions and some on college campuses. So the parts have been tested but not the whole. I have used a training program similar to the one outlined in Chapter 10. It works. I have listened in on a discussion between a man and his manager quite similar to the sample in Chapter 11. Both parties said it was a helpful and satisfying talk.

I haven't relied on my judgment alone on the special cases described in Chapters 6, 7, 8, and 9. Many of the ideas suggested were contributed by and reviewed with representative individuals of the category discussed.

I recognize that this book is only a beginning. The subject of career management needs further probing and a great deal of experimentation. I hope the reader is encouraged to do both.

Marion S. Kellogg

Contents

1 **Career Systems Must Change**   1
Decentralization: A Key Factor—Imprecise Prediction—New Challenges

2 **Manpower Planning Versus Career Management**   14
Business Plans and Manpower Plans—Personnel Evaluation—Plans for Promotable Individuals—Career Management—Procedures Needed—Interpretive Communication—Personal Skills—A More Comprehensive System

3 **The Individual's Role: Career Managing**   28
Steps in Career Management—The Employee's Responsibilities

4 **Management's Role: Facilitating**   43
No Tokenism—No Manipulation— Good Jobs—Good Bosses—Educational Opportunities—A Working Promotion System—Business Information—Career Shifts—Reevaluate Five- to Ten-Year Men

5 **Equal Treatment of Employees and Applicants**   57
Obstacles in the Promotion System—Opening Up the Promotion System

6 **A Fast Start for Young Employees**   75
Screening and Monitoring First Jobs—Finding Men Who Make Good First Bosses—Testing Reality to

CONTENTS

Learn About the Work World—Providing Reinforcement and Feedback—Tracking Attitudes of New Employees—Dealing with Confrontations

7 Advancing Careers of Minority Professionals 93
Costly Errors and Omissions in Minority Career Development—Advancement for the Minority Professional

8 Women and Career Opportunities 108
The Facilitating Management Role—Career Management and Women's Responsibilities

9 Senior Employees 125
Facilitating the Older Employee's Career—Ways the Mature Employee Can Help Himself

10 A Manager Training Program 142
Outline of a Six-Session Training Program—Case Studies

11 A Sample Career Discussion 168
Case Study and Dialog—The Manager's Contribution

12 The Real World 186
Career Boosts—Career Barriers—An Overall Evaluation

1

Career Systems Must Change

"REASON for leaving: Better opportunity."

These words written on an exit inverview form are all too familiar to the personnel director faced with staffing problems. This is probably the most popular reason for resignations, and it is often given by the more competent and productive employees—the ones we hate to lose. It is just one of the results of narrowly conceived and too long neglected career-planning and promotion systems for professional, supervisory, and management personnel.

In view of this fact, it is surprising that these systems remain so underdeveloped. It is especially surprising at this point in management history, when the need to apply Douglas McGregor's Theory Y is so widely proclaimed and when words like "trust" and "openness" are heard at every conference on leadership. If we are to obtain the benefits of individual satisfaction coupled with substantial management continuity, the vitally important factors of career-planning systems can no longer be given perfunctory attention.

It's hard to find anyone who is satisfied with the present state of affairs. Personnel specialists see current inadequacies clearly. One management development executive says: "We have a pretty good set of promotion rules here, but if a manager makes up his mind to put Joe Doakes into a job, one way or another he does it." Another says: "The appraisal data we collect on employees are just worthless. Some managers won't say anything critical; others won't say anything specific; we put it in the record, but it doesn't mean a thing." Still another says: "We don't find out about an opening until it's too late."

Presidents of corporations talk about the need for top talent to fill prospective executive positions while within their firms capable men and women are frustrated in their attempts to move up the ladder. Managers who have been around for a while feel they are bypassed in favor of younger men. Young people cry foul in two instances. If the institution with which they're affiliated is active in moving employees around in order to broaden experience, they may claim their privacy is invaded, their right to manage their own lives is threatened, or they are victims of a manipulative system. If, on the other hand, companies follow a cream-will-rise-to-the-top policy, they say industry is uncaring and abandons its human responsibilities.

When promotion systems are opened to professional scrutiny, in fact, the knowledge barriers inherent in prediction, the lack of sound career philosophies, the gap between a firm's intentions and its effect, and many short-term expediencies all become glaringly apparent. In addition, the inadequacies of business planning, our poor ability to understand and define job requirements systematically, and our adult education failures are reminders of the good game we talk but fail to play. Of all the problems, the knowledge barrier is the most serious. It emphasizes the need for experimentation to find out what is effective in today's and tomorrow's setting. Experimentation in the career area, however, takes courage, imagination, and funding—elements singularly lacking in most manpower development programs.

Why are we in such a predicament? What has been happening in recent years to deepen the need for resolving career advancement problems?

Decentralization: A Key Factor

First of all, most institutions have grown, and with increased size have come organization changes, notably toward decentralization. While decentralization solves some problems, it is not a panacea, and it generates some obvious hazards. The president (or general manager or managing director—whatever his title may be) has less opportunity to know the talents of the young comers. He is often at the mercy of lower-level managers who may in fact be concealing good men in their efforts to meet their clearly defined objectives. These young men may hold positions that fit their talents well. They may be developing at a normal rate. But they may not be moving to new assignments soon enough to satisfy them, to accelerate their rate of growth and broaden them for different and more important future positions.

Second, corporate systems designed to overcome this problem by systematically identifying high-potential men and developing individual career plans for them are difficult to enforce. ("How can I meet the very tough objectives I've agreed to if you take my best man away at just this moment?" is a typical conversation stopper.) Such systems tend to bog down in paperwork. ("All I know is that all these forms arrived with a note from topside saying that they should be completed and returned within a month. We did it, got a lot of people excited about it, and sent them in, and nothing has happened since.") They offer, moreover, little or no reward for managers who do their development homework and supply talent to other departments of the enterprise. ("Why should I give up good men? All top management looks at is the figure in the lower right-hand corner of the balance sheet!")

First Job, First Boss

Another enduring problem that is intensified in decentralized operations is early identification of top performers. Much of the so-called promise of workers is deduced from how they do on early assignments. But the nature of the work delegated to a man and the supervisor or manager to whom he reports are significant determinants of the extent of promise or potential that he can reveal. Just as some quite brilliant students are turned off by the lack of challenge they find in the schoolroom, so very capable people may appear uninterested and sluggish and perform no better than average because of the unchallenging work they are asked to do, the low-level standards of the manager, or the kind of environment in which they work.

Managers often suffer from feelings such as these: "I did the dull stuff in the beginning; so can everyone else." "You only get ahead if you learn the business from the bottom up." "Reading instruments may not be exciting, but somebody's got to do it." "It's time you learned there's no such thing as a perfect job." To be fair, we must acknowledge that few recognize their own attitudes for what they are. They are so ingrained that these managers no longer stop to analyze them. But think of their effect on a bright, well-trained young man trying to find himself in a strange world. He may say to himself: "In this company, it doesn't matter what I know or know how to do. I've got to do a certain amount of drudgery just to meet the requirements of the system." Work becomes meaningless to him; he doesn't identify with it at all. Or if he shows some spunk and asks "Why?" when he's told to do it, he is labeled difficult to get along with from that time on.

It is important not to overlook the fact that the foreman, supervisor, or manager at the bottom of the pyramid is often in one of two career stages himself. He may be a hotshot, moving ahead rapidly. In this case, he is probably inexperienced and self-centered and thus unconcerned about the motivational needs of others in the organization. Or he may have plateaued at this level, so that his own upward movement is unlikely or rather far in the future. In this case, he may well view those who report to him through his own perspectives. He may judge capabilities and contribution in terms of his own. He may expect very little and never get close enough to employees to see that they have much more to give.

It is rare indeed that a first job and a first boss are both such that they bring out the best in a person. When we realize that a new college graduate is struggling to build an image for himself—of what he is and can be—in his new setting, the critical nature of this early experience becomes apparent. Psychologists tell us a person refines his image by testing the limits of a situation in various ways. The responses that come from these test probes tell him whether he fits, whether he can give what is needed. If the image is good in his view, he shapes or molds himself to it; or if he finds the demands incompatible with his values, he drops out of the race or changes jobs. Thus, from both the organization's point of view and the man's, this first job may well be the key job of his career.

Outmoded Administrative Practices

Our personnel practices and benefit plans support a concept of career building that is archaic. As employee education level and job specialization have increased in all our institutions, the number of professional workers has grown. The marks of a professional are his independence of thought, his desire to set high standards for himself, and his persistent and aggressive push for freedom to work where his specialty is in demand. The professional has always advocated doing his own thing. But salary, which correlates more with length of service than with any other factor; promotion schemes that insist on a man's going through a certain number or set of musical chairs; and benefit plans that tie security, vacations, and other rewards to remaining with a firm all damp single-minded dedication to career specialization. Perhaps this is one reason for the large increase in consulting firms and indeed of independent consultants within the past decade.

At the very least, these factors tempt the individual to let go the reins of self-direction and encourage him to abdicate his career fulfillment to his company. The fact that management may not actively seek this responsibility is immaterial.

Self-fulfilling Prophecy

The hazards involved in coupling strong development programs with promotion systems are pretty well understood. If crown prince tactics are used—that is, if systematic methods are put into practice for identifying the most promotable employees and are followed by special training, information, and job assignments—history tells us that a high percentage of those selected will succeed in taking on higher-level managerial or specialist positions. Is it because they have been given so much additional experience that they become in fact better qualified than those not so treated? Is it that the display of confidence and support operates Pygmalion fashion stimulating them to undertake their work with greater confidence and a greater determination to live up to expectations?[1] Could it be that having identified these men and invested heavily in them, we convince ourselves of their superiority and screen out all but the most blatant signals of failure? Do other, equally capable employees, not so selected and trained, perceive the odds against them to be too great and move on to a new environment that gives them a better chance? These are the troublesome questions posed by a highly selective development and promotion system.

No Crown Princes

If the hazards of a crown prince system are great, those inherent in an equal-opportunity-for-all philosophy can be worse. The length of time taken to fill openings may be excessive because inadequate attention has been given to back-up support. Transition time can become overextended and thus detrimental to business. For example, if a man is chosen from another part of the firm, he may have to find his way in a new field or a new industry. He must learn about customers, competitors, organization and product strengths, and similar factors. In the course of learning, he may make costly strategic mistakes.

[1] See J. Sterling Livingston, "Pygmalion in Management," *Harvard Business Review*, July–August 1969.

CAREER MANAGEMENT

The theory of equal opportunity for all can in fact limit opportunity and increase specialization. To avoid the lengthy transition period, people are more and more often selected from within the organization. This excludes from consideration a wide range of capable people and perpetuates the design of steep, narrow careers so limiting at top levels. Training, too, becomes quite specialized if it is available to all because, as a practical matter, it will tend to focus on the product or output or specific needs of a given group. If attempts are made to broaden training but keep it available to all, it becomes expensive and administratively unwieldy. Most organizations seeking the best of both worlds settle for some combination of crown prince and equal treatment. Few if any are happy with the results. The point of course is that as long as job openings are primarily filled according to an institutional promotion system and employees as individuals have little access to the process, an unsatisfactory situation continues.

Imprecise Prediction

Decentralization, then, has contributed directly or indirectly to problems in career advancement. A second major source of difficulty is business planning. That all prediction is imprecise is not a new thought. What is new is that the rapid rate of change experienced in technology has added complexity to the problem. On the one hand, the availability of new products and services has opened new markets, so that decision making with respect to a business 5 to 10 or even 20 years hence requires more imaginative assumptions and choices than ever before. On the other hand, the computer provides a tool with which to generate data in answer to the question "What if . . . ?" Most executives are not prepared for either development.

Yet business planning and manpower planning, together with their offshoot career planning, are interdependent. The availability of human resources may well determine in large measure what a firm should undertake in the future. And manpower planning cannot be done adequately unless business plans are sound and based on expected events that do in fact come to pass. Both areas are fraught with assumptions that need to be monitored, and plans will have to be adjusted accordingly.

Since the record for prediction is not outstandingly good, all those involved in the total planning process need to understand what they are up against. In its simplest terms, estimating a person's potential within a given firm means looking ahead for a prescribed period of time, say, 5 or 10 years; identifying at least in broad outline the kinds of opportunities that will exist at that time, as well as critical environmental factors—political, economic, and social—that will make the work easy or hard to do; and finally, predicting how the person's talents and interests will have matured during the intervening years. The likelihood of our being able to do this soon with any degree of accuracy is remote.

In view of the uncertainty of both business and manpower forecasts, particularly when applied to a given individual or relatively small group of people, career planning must ethically be considered a joint venture. The employee must take part in the decision making, and his decision must be based on knowledge of the projected plans and the major assumptions that have been factored into them. In this way, he as well as the firm is in a position to monitor the accuracy of the predictions and adjust or adapt as is needed.

CAREER MANAGEMENT

New Challenges

A number of special areas challenge us today in career planning: culturally deprived minorities, women workers, demands of young people, and the shift in age distribution, to name some of the more important. Let's look at the nature of each of these problems.

Culturally deprived minorities. In the United States, laws prohibit discrimination based on race, creed, color, sex, age, or national origin. Both public and private moneys have contributed to training programs to teach skills to so-called hardcore unemployables. But as one Job Corps placement officer says: "We can train people, but this doesn't necessarily make them employable!" At best, it provides an entrée to work. To stay in the job once obtained requires more than skill. It requires good work habits, team contribution, a view of one's job in the perspective of others it touches—in fact, life habits that adapt to the regimen of organized daily work. To help the minority worker acquire these characteristics involves long-range, complicated interaction with him—one that we do not yet understand. But to obtain and keep a first job is hardly the American dream. The old dream (and there is no reason to suppose that it has died) is to have the opportunity to advance at least a little way up the ladder. So the career advancement problem (barely explored, much less resolved) of the minority worker shares the limelight with employability on a modest basis now, but it will surely gain increasing significance in the years ahead. Its resolution will contribute much to the satisfactory outcome of the ongoing social revolution.

Women. The most common reason firms give for failing to employ women or to consider them seriously for promotion opportunities is that they will leave to marry, to have a child, or to follow their husbands to a new career opportunity in a different geographic location. A number of things are happening to play down the validity of this argument. First, there appears to be a trend toward greater mobility among males, so that the relative position of men and women is now more even. Second, changes in social mores and values have contributed to the desire and need for married women to remain in the workforce. Third, both fear of overpopulation and improved understanding of birth control methods have decreased the birth rate. But while the trend is down, nevertheless, from a career standpoint, the typical woman worker probably must plan for an interrupted career. This poses problems for her and for the organization she joins. Yet the law says: "No discrimination."

In addition, the psychological problem of men reporting to women must be faced and resolved by both sexes if promotions are to be available equally. Fortunately, the trends toward greater democracy and participation in managing bode well. And the concept of the manager's role that plays down its ascendancy should not only help the woman to assume managerial rank but also allow her to achieve stature and full rewards as a professional contributor as well.

Demands of young people. The rate at which we are adding information in all fields, the improvements in teaching methods, and the multiplicity of communications media are helping to provide the young college graduate entering the workforce with greater knowledge qualifications than ever before. He also brings with him impatience, a cavalier attitude toward long-standing policies, a questioning mind, and nonacceptance of many of the working values of an earlier age. Young people place greater emphasis on human relationships than did previous generations. They expect more of their employers. They look upon their careers as means of realizing their potential. But many do not see work as a 24-hour-a-day responsibility; they do not see a single employer as deserving of lifelong loyalty unless it serves their interests. They are quite accustomed to thinking in terms of world opportunity, and they are less tied to a single geographic location. Frequently the product of a broken home, they place a high value on and expect to work toward a close, meaningful marital relationship. Therefore they won't buy the 24-hour-a-day job. And so their work habits are likely to be different from those of people in the current workforce. This poses problems for them and for their employers. New systems are needed to release their great capabilities for useful results and to help them achieve that first promotion quickly and soundly.

Age distribution shift. If the knowledge explosion gives the young person an advantage, it certainly places the older worker at a disadvantage. His obsolescence is more rapid than ever. The ideal of a career in which the individual continuously assumes greater and greater responsibility until finally he retires in a blaze of glory and at the peak of his powers was perhaps never true. But today it has become even less likely. Just keeping pace means a lifetime educational effort. How will employers handle this? Will managers expect less effort on the job? Give more part-time training? Add to the employee's benefits package a training period each year or a sabbatical for updating his knowledge and abilities? Should career thinking be changed so that employees typically reach their peak at some middle-age level and then after a period of time drop back to a lower-level plateau without loss of face or prestige?

Many management theorists today recommend multiple careers as the only satisfactory solution to the problem—"multiple" meaning a career that encompasses several phases, each involving fairly dramatic change. Perhaps the first 20 years might be spent in the more competitive business and industrial settings; the next 10 in some independent staff, consulting, or professional role; and the last span of time in more humanitarian, less competitive arenas. Whether or not this solution is a viable one for most employed persons, the need certainly exists to fight obsolescence and adopt career patterns more suited to the times.

All these factors—increasing institutional size and decentralization of decision making, more complex business planning interrelated with manpower planning, and the many special challenges that face us today—point clearly to the desirability of a major overhaul of career systems. We sorely need new concepts to give both the individual and the firm greater flexibility. We need a sharing of responsibilities by all involved parties. And most of all, we need ingenious devices to facilitate careers so that talents can be applied and developed at the rate demanded by our challenging times.

2

Manpower Planning Versus Career Management

BEFORE proposing a new career system, let's look at the old one to be sure we understand the merits to be preserved as well as the deficiencies to be improved. Almost every firm does some form of manpower planning in order to insure its existence in the years ahead. Systems vary widely in their sophistication, formality, and administrative processes, but certain elements are fundamental and are found in most systems. These are

1. Translation of business plans into manpower needs.
2. Evaluation of individuals' talents and estimate of their potential.
3. Catalog of skills.
4. Manning tables or back-up charts.
5. Plans for promotable individuals.
6. Review and recycling of the process.

Manpower Planning Versus Career Management

Let's review how each of these is usually carried out and examine its adequacy.

Business Plans and Manpower Plans

Most companies periodically redefine the nature of their business, the value of their product or service, and their basic strategy. This is usually done by top management with specialized staff assistance. The projection into the future ranges from 5 to 20 years.

The vice-president of personnel or the personnel director is then given the task of estimating critical manpower needs based on business planning decisions. This involves him and his associates in exploring the many trends that affect people, their knowledge, skill, interests, life style, and availability. Such data can be found in government bulletins, publications of survey groups, foundations, educational institutions, and similar sources.[1] Based on available information, several judgments are made, usually projected from past experience, about the ability of the firm to attract and retain employees, the probable shifts in organization structure, the change in numbers and kinds of managerial talent, the need for special skills at professional and nonprofessional levels, changes in geographic location, and other factors that affect staffing requirements.

With the help of line managers, a rough timetable of the more important needed manpower actions is drawn up. It becomes a sort of master plan for adding or subtracting personnel, changing the mix of talent within the firm, introducing specialized training, and similar critical steps.

[1] See Eli Ginzberg, Dale L. Hiesland, and Beatrice G. Reubens, *The Pluralistic Economy* (New York: McGraw-Hill, 1965); *The Outlook for Technological Change and Employment,* prepared for the National Commission on Technology, Automation and Economic Progress, February 1966. Available from Superintendent of Documents, U.S. Government Printing Office, Washington, D.C. 20402.

CAREER MANAGEMENT

This process will probably continue into the foreseeable future. The computer may help explore alternatives of structure, talent mix, and the like so that apparently optimum choices can be made. As suggested earlier, this is an imprecise prediction at best. With it, however, progress can be measured against the planned targets and adjustments can be made as they're needed or desired. Without it, we don't know where we're going so we have no way of determining whether we're getting there.

Personnel Evaluation[2]

It is the difficult step of evaluation that halts the manpower planning process and keeps it from being the powerful tool it was designed to be. The personnel staff, holding the master personnel plan, wishes to know the extent to which current employees can be counted on to fill anticipated needs. Staff members usually devise a form, therefore, that the immediate manager or supervisor is asked to complete with the help of each employee. The form requests a mix of the employee's personal biographical data, work experience history, and career interests as well as a rating of his performance on his present job and of his potential. The last may call for one or more of several evaluations. Some forms ask for the most complex, responsible position the individual is likely to be able to hold successfully. Some want a rating of his immediate promotability. Others ask for his percentile position on a normal curve of promotability as compared with that of his associates. Still others request a rating of his ability to achieve one or more of his expressed career interests. Almost all seek descriptive information about the strengths and weak-

[2] Marion S. Kellogg, *Closing the Performance Gap* (AMA, 1967), Chap. 10.

nesses he would display in specified future jobs if he were to attain them.

The problem is that evaluation is not a process that managers are overly fond of—nor do they do it well. There is a great deal of paperwork if all the data are to be recorded. If the material is discussed with the employee, it is time-consuming at minimum. It may also force some managers to soften their evaluation, making it less accurate than is desirable. But if evaluations are not softened, they may well disturb some excellent workers, whose performance may deteriorate as a result or who may leave if they feel their careers will be limited by staying.

Now, we can say that business planning predictions are imprecise and that we can take care of the health of the business by adjusting and recycling them at suitable times. But when we are dealing with human beings whose lives are affected by procedures known to be imprecise, we cannot be so glib. Here is an area where either appraisals must be improved or their role in career advancement must be made less important. In view of current knowledge, the latter seems sounder.

Skills Catalog

If the firm is small, the basic data noted on the manpower planning form may be kept on file, or they may be coded and a mechanical system used for easy access. If the firm is of such size that data on all employees cannot be efficiently stored, only those considered promotable, most promotable, or promotable outside their current organization component are placed in the inventory. High-speed electronic storage and sorting systems may be used.

Most firms feel the storage system itself is adequate. But this method raises other problems needing solution:

1. Whose data should be stored?
2. What information should be stored?
3. How can it be kept up to date?
4. How can more accurate and relevant evaluative information be made available?
5. Who should have access to stored information?
6. Should the individual know whether he is in the inventory and what it says about him?

Manning Tables and Back-up Charts

To supplement the general manpower planning information, managers are often asked to prepare organization charts showing the present structure and the incumbents in all positions. They are asked in addition to list three individuals who are in their opinion best qualified to replace each incumbent. Some color or letter code is used to indicate either the degree of qualification of each back-up specified or the number of years it will take each to be ready for the job in question. A refinement of this practice is to ask the manager to prepare these charts not according to the present structure but as he anticipates it will be in, say, six months or one year.

This procedure suffers from the ills of all prediction, but still it appears to be a useful device for looking in depth at the organization. It becomes more powerful as the manager reviews it with the manager at the next higher level and as he repeats the process at regular intervals, probing reasons for changes, job placements that have not followed the indicated choice, and so on.

Solutions are needed, however, at least to the following problems: (1) Should the individual know he is or is not on the back-up chart? (2) Should he agree to his candidacy if he is named? (3) If he is aware of his candidacy for one or more positions, what should be done if he is not selected when an opening occurs?

Plans for Promotable Individuals

Logically, if a man is named as promotable to a substantially better position or series of positions, some plans should be made to prepare him. This responsibility is usually given his immediate manager alone or in conjunction with the next-higher manager. Sometimes a member of the personnel staff serves as a consultant. Experience shows that, left to the immediate manager only, the plans are unimaginative, usually consist solely of training, and are frequently not carried out. In the best situation, in which two levels of management work with the help of a personnel specialist, planned job moves are usually supplemented with training. These changes are more frequently implemented, although timetables do slip dramatically.

While planning could certainly be more imaginative, the practice is sound and should be continued and improved. The major problems are (1) How to get better participation and cooperation from the individual. (2) What to do about those for whom there are no plans and who may be as promotable as those so labeled. (3) How to conceive plans that will have a decidedly favorable impact on individual development.

Review and Recycling

Any system relying heavily on prediction must be reviewed and recycled to account for progress and actual events. So this phase must be retained. This means that business planning must be updated periodically, with changes implied for the master personnel plan noted, evaluation made current, and so on. But there would be much greater flexibility and many problems would be eliminated or minimized if the emphasis on the future in manpower planning could be brought into better balance with concerns for the present.

An Authoritarian System

What an authoritarian system it is! The individual has almost no role in it at all. He is mainly expected to respond, preferably favorably. Yet a fundamental expression of himself is involved here—his output, his work, his lifelong pursuit. T. M. Alfred labels the present system "checkers."[3] It serves the institutional purpose, presumably, and *some* employees benefit from it. But it is far from the joint venture it could be and far from McGregor's Management Theory Y. Moreover, it puts too many of the institution's eggs in one basket of dubious strength—the appraisal of performance and potential. The main point, however, is that it simply hasn't worked very well. Even when firms shore up various parts of the process with new or refined tools, most managers and personnel people admit its frequent failures.

Career Management

I propose a shift from this system to a practice more in keeping with the basic principles of self-determination and joint man-management effort, one that aligns corporate and per-

---

[3] See "Checkers or Choice in Manpower Management," *Harvard Business Review,* January–February 1967, p. 157.

sonal goals. The proposed system is *career management,* which preserves the freedom of the individual to direct his own life, to maintain essential responsibility for his career. It also preserves top management's right to plan its business, provide for continuity of management, and organize needed professional talent to meet corporate objectives.

How does career management work? To put it simply, the individual programs his own career, drawing on selected expertise and information. When he chooses to affiliate with a particular institution as the best way to meet his personal objectives, he cooperates fully with organization systems; yet he still is free to change his affiliation should his personal targets make this desirable. In turn, the institution completely opens its career systems to employee initiatives while retaining the right to select people for its open positions. Development programs designed for career advancement purposes are treated as joint man-management ventures. In order to make them work, certain prerequisites must be met. First of all, management and employees must share a basic career philosophy as well as a clear understanding of the role of each in staffing and in advancing individual careers. Next, procedures and devices must exist to make the philosophy a reality and not merely an ideal. Third, there must be sufficient communication so that participation by all concerned will be intelligent. Finally, both managers and professional employees must be given skills training to make their interaction effective. Let's look at a few ground rules for each of these.

Philosophy of Career Management

Under career management, an individual is responsible for directing his own career. When he elects to associate himself with an organization, he retains the right of choice with respect to any action that has his career as its primary focus. This means he must know about an action and must agree to it if it is taken by the institution. If he disagrees with it, he must then take steps to protect his own interests. This may mean anything from a change in position to a possible career setback or slowdown if he fails to make a change he believes wise.

Management is responsible for meeting its corporate objectives over both the short and the long range. This means it has the right and the responsibility to choose the individuals who staff the organization. It also has the right and the responsibility to offer training and other benefits or practices to prepare individuals for positions or help them to perform more effectively.

Out of respect for each other's rights and responsibilities, the man and the organization must meet certain obligations. The employee must be sure that his accomplishment level demonstrates his abilities. He must also communicate his career interests to management in specific terms as well as the reasons for his agreement or disagreement with proposed actions that affect his plans.

Management must put facilitating systems in motion for filling open jobs and for learning of the employee's accomplishments and his general and specific career interests. To the extent compatible with corporate objectives, such systems should also help advance the employee's career. In addition, full communication must be provided so that all employees can use all career-facilitating systems intelligently.

Practically speaking, a career for an employed person is one outcome of the relationship of the person with the institution. When the goals of the organization and those of the individual match *reasonably,* the individual's occupational growth follows the organization's closely. At the same time, his career evolves at a rate and in a direction that are the joint results of efforts by the managerial hierarchy above him and his own self-determining actions. The closer in the hierarchy a manager is to an individual, the more responsibility he has for assignment of work and, therefore, the greater is his developmental impact on the direction and rate of the man's career.

His is not the sole contribution, however. For the individual, in accepting the position reporting to this manager, deliberately remaining in his job, recommending and agreeing to work assignments, and experimenting (or not) with work methods, exercises his self-determination as he contributes substantially to the direction and rate of growth of his own career.

Procedures Needed

To make the philosophy meaningful, a firm must have a functioning promotion procedure that it communicates fully to all employees. It must establish rewards for managers who encourage employees to use the procedure and even greater rewards for those who are so successful in contributing to employee development that those under them who try for promotion are accepted quite frequently. Before managers can learn of employee interests in any meaningful way, they must be in a position to give information about possible new fields of work and future manpower needs stemming from the business plans of the firm. The manager may not have the skill to counsel on careers, but he must at least be prepared to transmit information successfully. If the firm is large enough, the personnel office may have people who can counsel employees on a professional basis or know of outside counselors on whom employees may call for guidance and unbiased suggestions.

CAREER MANAGEMENT

The individual retains his personal responsibility for advancing his career interests by seeking information (not waiting for it to be given) about the promotion system from his immediate manager or another designated person or group. He should also periodically seek unbiased professional counseling about possible directions for his career. The source may be inside the company or independent of it. Further, he should test his value from time to time with other firms, other kinds of institutions, and so on in order to determine whether his personal standards for progress are realistic. In making intelligent use of promotion procedures, the individual becomes in effect a program manager for his own career. He postulates targets, negotiates contributions from others, develops progress checks, and adjusts his program and schedule as he learns more about himself and his talents and as his values mature. Methods and skills for program management have been developed in defense businesses for major projects. Expertise is at a high level, so a man need not invent the process for himself.

Interpretive Communication

Communication between management and employees must not only be full; it must be interpretive as well. The mere description of how lists of candidates are prepared to fill openings, how the screening is conducted and who makes the final selection is just a skeleton of the information employees need. Interpretive communication tells not only how lists are prepared but at what time and by what process names are considered for inclusion in such a list. Do nominees come from current managers or do personnel placement specialists suggest them on the basis of employee records? Which are the access points from the employee's point of view? When and how should he make his interests and his desire known?

Is there only one channel, through his immediate manager, or are there alternate routes?

In the presentation of business plans to a given employee or work group it is not enough for a firm to describe new areas of effort. It should *interpret* the plans by pointing out the possible implications of the need for more management talent, greater market development skill, new technology needs, and the like. In other words, relevant points from the master personnel plan are made known. The communication is not only factual, then, but aimed rather precisely at those who, interested in career implications for themselves, will learn about them while those who give inadequate attention to the development of their careers will find their interest aroused.

On the employee side of the responsibility ledger, there are key initiatives to be taken. An employee has the obligation to express his career interests when they appear to be in consonance with those of the organization. He shouldn't wait for a system to be activated before doing this but should take the lead in this regard. When channels are designated, however, he should use them. If a format for doing so is prescribed, he should follow it. If part of the problem of the system is its lack of currency, he should assume the initiative to keep it up to date.

In return, the management system must keep the employee's confidence so that his career desires are known only to those he has previously agreed to inform. His expression of interest should be without penalty if it should be contrary to the interests of his present assignment or department.

Personal Skills

The philosophy, the procedures, and the communication are unlikely to be implemented by chance. At each step, individuals with all manner of personal styles and all degrees of personal ambition are involved, and their skills—their collective expression of behavior and attitude—determine in large measure the success of career management in the firm.

The president who espouses a philosophy and then gives it only lip service, always rewarding the most favorable profit and loss (P&L) situation, *may* be sincere, but he is certainly at best inept. He needs to develop recognition skills and practices that adequately reward performance in the career advancement area.

The manager who seeks information on employee interests must be an astute and sensitive interviewer. The manager who appraises performance and attempts to translate it into predictive trends must be aware of the potential inaccuracy of such forecasts as well as the possible negative effect on motivation.

The personnel officer who evolves and explains the promotion system must do so from the customer's viewpoint, the customer being not only the manager whose position needs to be filled but any employee who might want the job.

The employee who wishes consideration for a better job must learn how to present his qualifications and interests adequately. He must learn to demonstrate his abilities. He must learn how to interview and be interviewed. He must have skill in negotiating the terms under which he accepts a job when one is offered.

A More Comprehensive System

It should be clear that career management as described is not a simpler system than manpower planning. It adds complexity by increasing the responsibilities of all involved. It demands new tools and processes and therefore new skills on the part of those who use them.

Manpower Planning Versus Career Management

Most of the unanswered problems and questions of manpower planning can be circumvented if they're studied and the individual employee is given greater access to the system. Then he will know more about business plans and alternatives, participate in and take more responsibility for development beyond his current job, and be in a stronger, self-nominative position when openings occur.

We do not recommend that manpower planning be dropped but rather that the one-sidedness of the process be eliminated. At each stage of the process where a unilateral decision is usually made (based frequently on one-sided information as well), change it so as to give clear access to employees. The problem, of course, lies in making this access real with adequate vehicles for personal input. Mere lip service to an open system will only make matters worse, as will inordinate administrative burdens placed on management. The first step, then, is a more detailed delineation of the roles and responsibilities of the individual and the institution.

3

The Individual's Role: Career Managing

THE dictionary definition of "career" is "the course one's life takes in pursuit of a particular interest." In this text, discussion of careers is limited to the course of the working life of professional and management employees who are associated with business, industry, government organizations, and similar institutions. Can such careers be managed? A personal poll of about a dozen employees brought me these typical responses:

> For the most part, it's working hard and being in the right place at the right time.
>
> Mostly luck . . . but you have to be ready if it comes your way.
>
> You have to know what fields are going to open up and get into them early.

The Individual's Role: Career Managing

I guess it's *who* you know, but even then you can't be a complete dud.

A certain person was the biggest factor in my life.

Boy, there are so many things that can go wrong, I sometimes wonder how I've gotten as far as I have.

All these answers seem to imply that an individual has some control over what he knows and can do and over how hard he works. But they also seem to suggest that most people feel at the mercy of chance and pretty dependent on the help of others to get them into scoring position. No one denies the existence of luck. And no one can be professionally successful, in the generally accepted sense of the term, totally on his own. Even the artist needs a gallery to display his works, publicity to tell others about it, and, on a still more fundamental level, a supplier of paints, brushes, and other equipment to enable him to function. But to a far greater degree than most people recognize, careers can be managed, though this requires more attention, self-study, professional advice, and objective analysis than most managers or employees have given the matter so far.

Steps in Career Management

The notion that managing a career means controlling everything that happens must be abandoned. When we talk about managing an estate or managing a business, we recognize that many variables are out of control. What we do, however, is to establish a plan that appears reasonable in the light of current trends, implement it, form the relationships necessary to obtain needed contributions from others, watch progress carefully, keep an eye on external events, and recycle the plan periodically to keep it realistic and current. This process, successful in every other kind of management, can add substantially to success in achieving personal career goals. Let's examine several of these steps to understand their meaning for career management.

Establishing a Career Plan

For most individuals, a career plan consists of the intention to become a doctor, or to run a small business, or to be an engineer. In business, the equivalent of this would be, "We plan to make a profit." And just as the latter is totally inadequate to insure a successful business, so for the individual the general intention does little to achieve the desired result. If the plan is really to contribute to career success, it needs to be much more specific in describing the objective and in delineating a strategy for reaching it.

The preflight procedure performed by pilot and crew provides an interesting analogy. Even before a routine 200-mile flight, they have a checklist of items to inspect and must find them acceptable before takeoff is permitted. Why, then, on a unique mission such as the launching of a career, do most individuals give so little systematic attention to essential items that may make the difference between success and failure? The accompanying box provides a minimal checklist for self-examination. If the answers to these questions are yes, an individual must then make three decisions: What vocational path will he choose to begin with? What investment of time, effort, and money is required to be successful in it? Which general strategy will he follow to get into it and be successful in it? These decisions must be made in specific terms so that they truly guide the person's activities on the career front. Since they interrelate, none is made in isolation.

The Individual's Role: Career Managing

> **Career-launching Checklist**
>
> 1. Do I know the things I do best?
> 2. Have I found some things I like to do very much?
> 3. Do I work better by myself or with other people? What sorts of other people?
> 4. Do I know what talents I do not have?
> 5. Do I know the things I very much dislike doing?
> 6. Have I gotten professional advice on the fields of work I ought to consider for myself?
> 7. Does my education prepare me for these fields, or do I need further education or specialization courses or some sort of internship before making a full-fledged beginning?
> 8. How hard am I willing to work physically and mentally? Can I work long hours?
> 9. What are my work habits? Short bursts of very intense effort? Or a steady pace?
> 10. Have I talked with people doing jobs I think I might or should be interested in so that I have first-hand information on what they do, how they do it, and what a typical day is like for them?

For example, consider the case of John X. He has reached his fourth year of college with a mechanical engineering major. He has already learned through discussions with his professors that he is not an ingenious designer or gadgeteer. His math, while adequate, is not a great strength. He depends on other people and urgent problems to arouse his interest and challenge his competitive spirit. He talks to as many mechanical engineers as he can to find out what different kinds of work are open to someone with training in mechanical engineering. With the additional help of the college placement director, he rules out research, development, and design because of his mathematical weakness, his lack of ingenuity, and his need for people and short-term problem stimulus. On the basis of all these discussions, he lists consulting engineering, application engineering, shop or production engineering, and sales engineering as possibilities.

When our hypothetical engineer considers how much time and effort he is willing to invest, he decides that consulting engineering would take more time away from home and longer hours than he is willing to give right now. Further, consulting work would involve the development of specialties that could mean a number of years of hard work and quite possibly specialized courses as well. He is unwilling to make these investments at this time. Applications, sales, and production engineering appear to be reasonable choices.

As for skills, all three areas would require John to have some design experience to become thoroughly familiar with the product. Since his design talents are not strong, he feels he will probably be successful only if the product is relatively simple. On the other hand, it must be sufficiently complex that applications work will be important and that the shop will have problems requiring engineering attention. The size of the firm is important, too. It must be large enough to have an engineering organization with engineering specialties.

John then considers the jobs toward which these specialties are likely to lead. He talks to two personnel directors and learns that applications work usually leads to sales and then to sales management. Shop engineering, on the other hand, probably develops into manufacturing management. With this information in mind, he talks to as many people as possible in both kinds of work. He learns that manufacturing is likely to involve long hours (which he doesn't want) and much pressure because of relatively short-term emergencies (which he likes). Sales management has more freedom (which he likes) but probably involves extended work days (which don't appeal to him) with quite a bit of social pressure (which he doesn't like). Weighing all the factors and recognizing he cannot have everything he wants, he concludes that he will probably do better in production or shop engineering and enjoy it more and that he can hope it will lead him into manufacturing management. Acting on this decision, he develops plans for finding the initial position.

Implementing a Career Plan

Once the objective has been determined, action must be taken to obtain a suitable first job in which a man can demonstrate his talents. With the help of vocational counselors, college placement directors, and similar professionals, John X. identifies likely organizations and lays out a campaign for presenting credentials, meeting representatives involved in the hiring and placement process, and finding suitable existing openings for which to compete. Such a campaign includes writing letters, visiting local firms, seeking interviews with traveling recruiters, placing and answering want ads, and working with agencies and management consulting firms.

An individual should seek professional help in writing résumés and ads and in presenting his qualifications in a letter or interview. These are skill areas that usually require a little practice, so the astute individual goes out on interviews and answers ads for jobs of marginal interest just for the experience.

In John's case, he draws up, with the help of his college placement director, a list of companies of about the right size and with products that seem to meet his specifications. He prepares his résumé and slants the covering letter to reflect both his immediate and his longer-term job interests. He includes two or three items from his résumé that emphasize the strengths he would bring to a shop engineering position. He writes companies not interviewing on campus; he signs up to see representatives of others who are making the recruiting rounds.

Obtaining a desirable job does not complete the plan. If a career is in mind, the plan should include actions at least up to the first review point. Additional steps should be taken to make a smooth transition and a success of the job. These may well include obtaining sound information about the company or organization joined, acquiring good product and service knowledge, continuing courses to improve one's knowledge and skill, and getting a better grasp of the organization structure and information about the people who man it. These steps certainly must include the development of a plan (with the help of the new boss) to be sure assigned work is carried out with excellence.

Obtaining the Contribution of Others

Managing a career requires careful programming of information from other people. This means identifying the sorts of information you do not have and finding the sources and avenues of obtaining it. It also means learning how systems function, and which procedures or instructions must be followed, and how to follow them most effectively. Further, career management requires that you identify influential people and determine how to demonstrate your talents and interests to them. In the example, John needed suggestions of likely employers from the placement director. He also needed information from men doing the kinds of work he was considering and advice from interested interviewers to help him reexamine the assumptions he had made about his qualifications.

The Individual's Role: Career Managing

Once on the job, he will need feedback from his manager to help him perform well, as well as help from his associates.

Such help is not often volunteered. Disinterested third parties must have their interest aroused. Special efforts need to be made to find common ground with them, to involve them in planning when possible, and occasionally tradeoffs should be offered. There are some ground rules for obtaining help from others.

1. Ask for it. No one can read your mind. If you need something from someone, make the need known.
2. Be sure he understands why you want it and how important it is to you. The vague, general request often produces no result, so be explicit in stating what you want, how you plan to use it, and what its use will do for you. If you have a time limit, say so.
3. Ask the right person. Don't go around someone or over his head or ask someone not responsible for the matter to do you a favor.
4. Don't impose. Don't ask for more than the person has a responsibility for giving.
5. Follow up. If time is short, ask in advance whether the request will be met on time. But don't nag. There is a nice balance between displaying interest in the result and following up every few minutes in an obnoxious manner.
6. Thank him when he produces. If the effort was unusual, make sure his boss knows what he did.

Monitoring Progress

No plan is worthy of the name without some milestones along the way. Dates for career plans may not be quite so definite as those for product developments, but they can at least specify the first six-month period during which progress will be reviewed and assumptions examined.

In John's case, it will probably be two years before he takes his first serious look. Has he gotten past the preparatory position in design engineering and been selected for a shop engineering assignment? Does he like the work and find it satisfying? Are the pressures and short-term problems challenging? What about the company he has chosen, and the people for whom and with whom he works? Do choices for the future appear as he thought they would, or are new opportunities evolving?

In addition to answering these questions, a person should turn back to the career-launching checklist to be sure he is adding to his knowledge about his working self. He should rethink his three fundamental decisions and, on the basis of his answers, revise his action plans.

The Employee's Responsibilities

It should be obvious that each person must carry out this kind of management process for his own career. To yield the programming to someone else is to abandon responsibility for one's life and one's contribution to society. However, to try to do it alone, to fail to elicit the informative help of others, is to live in an unreal world. To remain the passive object of others' actions is no solution either. While all around us there are pressures that help or hinder, that draw us toward or away from a particular course of action, in the end each individual must take the responsibility for deciding to respond or not, to take action or not, and thus reassert his essential responsibility for his life. Let's look at the specifics of personal responsibilities for career management.

The Individual's Role: Career Managing

Self-evaluation

The charge to "Know thyself" is hardly a new idea. Today, with the testing and counseling services available in high schools and colleges, in the military and the service organizations, and in business and industry, it is easy to think that it is the responsibility of such services to open our eyes to our abilities and to let our employer know how our talents can best be used in his firm. Instead, the individual should take and keep the initiative. If a man is to manage his career to his best advantage, he will view the suggestions and evaluations of others as useful information to be considered in the light of his own awareness of his strengths and interests. Weighing the total information puts him in a position to decide among the career choices open to him.

How should an individual make a self-evaluation? Fortunately, the things we like to do are usually things we do well. Start by taking a blank piece of paper divided by a line down the center. Put strengths on which to build a career on one side and deficiencies in talent on the other. Next, list courses you liked best and least and job duties you especially enjoyed or disliked greatly. Add community work and extracurricular activities you accomplished well and those you didn't.

Then think about the circumstances that surrounded some of the things you've listed as pluses. Were there certain kinds of people who helped make them pleasurable? Were you working pretty independently or tied closely to a team effort? Did you have loose or tight time limits? Were there any other factors that contributed to your pleasure in accomplishment? Do the same thing with the negatives. Is there a common thread to be aware of? Do you work best with certain kinds of people and under certain conditions? These matters can be important in making decisions.

You probably can't weigh the picture objectively. The probing, evaluations, and observations of others can help you. Possible sources include school placement counselors, past and present employers, personnel officers, management consultants, market and economic forecasters, and trends indicated in classified ads. It's important to find people with an awareness of likely growth areas in business, industry, and government. The issue is *not* simply what fields you are suited for but what growth areas could use your kinds of talents. Timing is important, too. Preferably, the peak demand for your talents should occur at about the time you have acquired experience and your talents have matured. Thus, matching your assets to growth fields is the key to much of career progress. Naturally, the match is seldom perfect, but with some adaptation and adjustments, it can provide a strong career objective.

Remaking the Job Choice

The choice of a position is not something one makes only when one begins a career or is tired of a job and wants a change or even when one is out of work and needs income. The decision should be remade each day—deliberately. Is it wise for me to be in this job today? Is it the most reasonable compromise with the ideal that can be made? Such a renewal of job choice does much to refresh energies and to refocus efforts toward career objectives. The opposite course—resigning oneself to the current situation until something forces a different decision—can be disastrous. It can lead to pedestrian work and to loss of self-respect and self-confidence. It encourages career floating and overreliance on one's employer or on an economic situation or some other external condition.

On the other hand, frequent renewal of the job decision forces an individual to weigh alternatives and, if the present position is best, all things considered, to identify why this is the case and capitalize on it. The rethinking of experience or skill needs may call for a second look at work underway to determine if it is being exploited fully. This can bring a fresh approach to work and may well force a change in work methods, results, and timing.

Knowledge of the Enterprise

It is not enough to grasp assigned job duties. Growth lies in understanding what the institution—the business or industry or organization—is all about. What is its purpose? What markets does it serve? What do its customers or clients value? This evaluation allows a view of one's work from an important perspective. It means a greater realization of what the manager above you does or should want and need. It means seeing your mission not only from your standpoint but from above and from the outside looking in. This new view invariably influences ways, means, and results so that these become more meaningful for the corporation. The successful career manager takes the initiative to find out about the total business. He can't wait until someone remembers to tell him about it. He does his homework with annual reports and similar documents. He asks questions and goes to informative meetings.

High Work Standards

When you renew your decision to remain in your position and study its contribution to your career advancement, looking at it from the perspective of market and customer values as if you were the owner-manager, your standards are changed and raised in subtle yet visible ways. Association with others doing similar work helps you adjust your standards to current professional levels as well. Meetings of trade associations, professional seminars, and the like all contribute information by which your standards evolve. Books in the field assist in the process. Improved contribution should be the result.

The Importance of Work Relationships

Relationships with associates, whether above, below, or at the same level in the organization, are the key to much of current and future success in all work efforts. Today's complex jobs demand contributions from many others besides oneself. A failure to obtain this contribution clearly limits one's growth.

Review and Reorientation

Each of us needs to sit down periodically and quietly evaluate where we are, what we have learned from our various experiences, and what the learning has meant to us. Is the measure of growth sufficient? Or have we let experiences wash over us without touching us significantly? And if we have made the most of our experiences, has it changed the target or the timing of our career efforts?

Flexibility

In spite of our best efforts to know ourselves and to set our career paths in reasonable directions, it often happens that new fields open up rather dramatically and unexpectedly. If we are managing our careers capably, we should be on the alert for such new opportunities and flexible enough to pursue them.

The Need for Special Help

When asked about their success, top executives frequently mention the contributions of former managers or associates.

These may have served as models. They may have aroused interest along certain lines. Perhaps they encouraged or discouraged the investment of effort in certain career directions. They might have held high expectations and displayed great confidence.

There are certain instances, moreover, in which individuals are greatly in need of help from others. Recognizing this fact early and deliberately seeking such help are important.

The uncertain man. Many men even of mature age are remarkably uncertain of what they would like to do with their lives. This uncertainty may arise because they have little talent or too many talents or because their energies are so diverted by personal defenses that there is little energy left for fundamental decision making.

Early in his career the uncertain man needs to seek the advice of professional guidance counselors or personnel placement specialists. He should be cautious about the qualifications of such people. But if their credentials are substantial, it's probably a safe beginning to follow their advice to a reasonable extent. As the career unfolds, periodic suggestions should also be sought.

This individual should investigate these professionals and talk to more than one to be sure he is on the right track.

The overly ambitious man. The overly ambitious man is even more dependent on external feedback. He is perhaps too confident of his own abilities; he doesn't want to live with his decisions; he wants to move ahead now, whatever costs may be involved. His relationships often suffer because of his vigorous pursuit of personal interests. He needs a strong manager with very high standards, one whom he respects and to whom he will listen.

The timid man. The timid man may feel he never knows enough or has had enough experience to be ready for more responsibility. He needs to chose a boss who does trust him and who may push him ahead faster than he feels he is ready to go.

The inflexible man. A man who sees only one way to do things may find himself terribly limited by his narrow view. He needs to pick people to work with who are spontaneous and creative and who will refuse to accept his set ways, people who will in fact laugh at him if he persists in clinging to outmoded or inferior work methods.

Another form of rigidity shows up in the man who sets his career course and makes up a timetable as we have recommended. But as his work progresses, he becomes overly concerned if he doesn't meet his scheduled objectives. He must recognize that timetables and directions are only approximations and need to be viewed with reason. If such a man finds that after a year in one position he hasn't yet moved to a new one, he shouldn't make rash moves. He should put himself on probation instead and say, in effect, "From now on I'll be alert to opportunities. Nothing hasty, but within the next six or eight months I should make a move." It would be advisable for him to seek an unbiased third party to counsel him and verify his thinking.

In short, then, an individual can be his own career manager. He outlines his targets, embarks on a reasonable course of action, and develops and displays his talents to a maximum extent. But he does not function in isolation. He seeks helpful contributions: personal examples, work assignments, counsel and reactions from others. If he chooses to join an organization, he alerts himself to its promotion system and makes full use of it.

4

Management's Role: Facilitating

IF the employee must be the master programmer for his career, if his own decisions necessarily come first because only he can apply his personal values effectively, what role does institutional management play? And how important is it?

Clearly, management's function is important. Employees and prospective employees have their own high levels of expectation about this. The consequences of failing to demonstrate positive, supportive interest in employee careers can be serious. In order to attract well-qualified talent in this age, when so many choices are open to professional and management people, long-term interest rather than short-term exploitation must be demonstrated. An informal survey of 100 seniors at a major university indicates that one of the attractions of any institution is the opportunity for career advancement that it offers. And exit interviews in employment offices still indicate that the main reason for voluntary resignations is lack of opportunity.

So, whether or not an individual takes advantage of career development programs within a firm, their presence attracts top talent.

No Tokenism

Lip service will not suffice. A pet peeve of both employees and undergraduates is career tokenism on the part of an organization. For example, some firms advertise a computerized inventory that stores data about current employees and is much publicized as the vehicle for filling open jobs fairly, giving equal opportunity to all qualified candidates. But when the computer is seldom used, when data are obsolete and little effort is made to keep them current, many consider this tokenism. When an enormous paperwork system is put into effect and career interests are solicited once a year and passed up the line for further review and consideration *but nothing else happens,* employees consider it tokenism.

No Manipulation

Employees want an open system. They want to know how jobs are filled and what the ground rules are for getting them. They bitterly resent being told they are free to accept or reject an offer of advancement, only to discover that if they reject it, either they are pressured to change their decision or they're rarely offered another opportunity. They dislike having their titles changed, their job descriptions rewritten, and their salaries increased modestly, and then finding they are doing the same work as before. They dislike being diverted to a different job in another department under the guise of helping out temporarily only to discover they're in a job they'd rather not be doing and the only other choice is to leave the firm. They especially resent the poorer performer's being given an opportunity for a better job because the boss wants to get rid of him, while stronger contributors are held in place. Employees want to be involved in their own career decisions with both the facts and the risks exposed.

So with those provisos—no tokenism, no manipulation—employees expect management to play an important role in career advancement. The nature of its role is best described as facilitating. Workers expect good jobs, bosses from whom they can learn, educational opportunities, a working promotion system, and sufficient information about the business. These are fundamental and deserve individual discussion.

Good Jobs

A good job is one reasonably matched to the knowledge, skills, and interests of the man who fills it. It must not be so much within his capability that he feels unchallenged by it. Rather, it should build on his talents and require him to stretch, thus adding to his knowledge and skill. Learning time must not be so long that a man becomes discouraged nor so short that within three or four months he has milked a job of its major learning potential.

The way the job is delegated is also critical. Management by objectives is strongly recommended so that the individual is working toward a result he's committed to and has considerable freedom to choose how he will reach it. He is aware of the constraints or limitations within which he must work, but these are not so severe and restrictive that the result seems impossible to attain. In addition, functioning within a management-by-objectives system provides him with automatic feedback so that he knows at all times how he is doing by comparing his progress with anticipated milestones.

The good job develops with the man. As he performs it and understands the work better, he sees opportunities to make improvements, to get results faster, or to get different and better results. Thus the learning opportunity increases with the experience of the man. A poor job is quite different. Early on, it is drained of its problems and challenges, so that the major learning experience for the individual is short-lived though it may be high. What follows takes on the coloration of routine—complex, perhaps, but repetitive.

In addition to the substance, depth, and increasing learning potential inherent in a good job, it also represents a course of action that matches the employee's interests at least to a reasonable extent and continues to arouse and stimulate them as time goes on. The job thus directly contributes to the advancement of his career.

But one mistake management often makes about the good job is to oversell it, describing the work in far more glowing terms than are realizable. To counteract any possible oversell, the prospective employee should spend enough time with the incumbent to see firsthand what he does and talk with associates involved with the work. If he can, he should try his hand at the work before accepting the job—perhaps an unrealistic possibility unless he's already employed by the firm.

Good Bosses

Employees expect to learn from their managers. This is often interpreted to mean that a manager knows so much

Management's Role: Facilitating

an employee will benefit from watching him work and from his explanations, coaching sessions, and performance appraisal discussions. It is now clear, however, that being a good boss is not quite so simple. In a survey I made a few years ago asking a group of young professional men under what type of manager they had grown most, the message came through clearly. It was not the personality of the man or what he did or didn't know that stood out. The developmental manager was one who had given them a tough job to do that was important to organization results and expected them to do it—no escape.

A good boss is one who not only provides freedom of operation but also sets a climate for the group that encourages each person to *take* the freedom he needs in order to operate successfully. Manager X., in working with one of his less confident engineers, keeps saying, "My door is always open. Don't hesitate to ask for my help. If you need help, advice, suggestions, you are always welcome to come, put your feet up, and talk things over." To the individual somewhat fearful of testing his wings, this seems fine. He comes frequently to his boss for advice. His manager is always warm and understanding and encouraging. "How can I help?" he asks, and the employee tells him. What Manager X. may be doing, probably with excellent intentions, is building dependence in the employee, whose decisions are never fully his own and whose risks are mainly shared. His work may be excellent, but Manager X. is not a good boss by career-advancement criteria.

Neither, of course, is Manager Y., who says, "When I give you a job, it's yours to do as best you can. I wouldn't ask you to do it if I thought it were impossible. But if you run into difficulty, well, join the club! Don't tell me your troubles; just get the job done." This abandonment of the managerial role and rejection of relationship responsibilities may prove developmental if the employee is thoroughly experienced and confident and is well on his way to top management. But to a beginner or a well-trained individual with little confidence, it may be a defeating tactic. The uninterested employee may just go on his merry way, planning to change jobs anyway should it appear he can't get results under existing conditions.

Manager Z. probably does better. He suggests that his experience, for whatever it may be worth, is available if needed. But the employee who comes constantly with problems is firmly and tactfully told to come with recommended solutions, and then only if there is a specific piece of information or action needed from the manager. He helps the employee build an upward relationship that should survive a variety of managerial styles.

Educational Opportunities

Most large companies spend large sums of money on training programs of all sorts. It is one of the advantages they offer. Company training programs, however, have a way of becoming stereotyped and no longer relevant to assigned work. A certain company, for example, may have given a course in electronic circuitry for 20 years. The current instructor has taught it for at least five years. The methodology, the problems, the course outline, and even the tests are completely standardized. Possibly the course gets a good rating by participants because the material is well organized, the instructor is reasonably effective, and there is no apparent basis for a poor rating, at least in the students' view.

But the most important reason for rating it down may

Management's Role: Facilitating

still be present: the material might be below the level of knowledge actually in use in the company. This can happen on the college campus as well as in the company classroom, of course, but the message is that if employees want educational opportunities for career advancement, they want fresh information, presented with the latest teaching methods.

Inviting university professors and gifted teachers to review subject matter and presentation methods can pay handsome dividends. Asking company specialists to audit course content to be sure of its currency can be enormously helpful. Bringing in prominent outside lecturers knowledgeable in the subject the course is treating can help break set patterns and open minds to fresh ideas. This brings better work results as well as facilitating employee career advancement. It may in fact save senior specialists from becoming obsolete.

Management need not do it all. Nearby institutions of learning may be encouraged to set up evening courses in subjects of interest. While many companies consider tuition refund an employee benefit in such instances, this isn't always necessary. Most employees are quite willing to pay their own way or share the cost involved. The object is to have outstanding learning opportunities readily accessible.

A Working Promotion System

A company sincerely interested in attracting and holding outstanding people must demonstrate convincingly that there is a promotion system in effect that is fair and that works to the common advantage of the employee and the company. There is no one system that is better than all others, but there are some essential features found in most.

CAREER MANAGEMENT

Stated Policy on Filling Openings

Here are some key questions to be answered.
1. Who has the decision-making responsibility for final selection? The manager alone, two levels of management, the manager with the concurrence of a personnel specialist?
2. Does this decision-making responsibility vary with the organization level (or salary level) of the opening?
3. How are candidate pools assembled? By the manager? By the personnel office? From inside the department, outside it, outside the company?
4. Who is eliminated from consideration? People of certain age groups, employees with short tenure in current jobs, employees rated below certain levels, those with specified health problems, those in certain parts of the organization?
5. Are some candidates given preference in consideration? Long-service employees, employees within the department where the opening occurs, those in specified training programs?
6. If an employee is selected, does he have the choice of accepting or declining without sacrificing future consideration?
7. If an employee is selected, does his present manager have the choice of permitting or refusing his acceptance?
8. If an employee is denied permission to accept, what recourse or appeal does he have?
9. Are the serious competitors for a position told of their status and of reasons for the final decision?
10. Are the monetary rewards and other perquisites attached to a position fixed and stated, or are they negotiable at the time of offer and acceptance?

If these questions are answered and published together with the reasons behind them, employees will understand the ground rules and will judge management on the consistency with which it lives up to stated policy.

Simple procedures in use to implement policy. A policy is only as good as the procedures and tools available to implement it. Regardless of the policy decisions, the following are needed:

1. *Notice of actual or impending opening.* This may be a form to be completed or a note or checklist of items to be included in the description of the responsibilities of the opening.

2. *Specifications for the opening.* The most useful is a list of things the incumbent should have done in the past, the conditions under which he should have functioned successfully, and the kinds of experiences that are most likely to have prepared him for the opening.

3. *Up-to-date personnel data records.* Some itemization is needed of current expressions of career interests and of the education, work experience, and extracurricular activities of all employees, assembled in a form that permits efficient search with elimination of unqualified individuals and identification of those to be considered. In large companies, this usually means some computerized sorting system. In smaller firms, a manual or mechanical sort is probably adequate.

4. *Evaluative tools.* Once the candidate pool is assembled, evaluative tools are needed to expose the full talents of the individuals involved. These may consist of past performance appraisals, past accomplishments matched against plans, personal interview data, tests, checks with former managers who know the individual's work and methods, and similar sources of information.

5. *Data comparison.* With the information about the leading contenders in hand, a systematic method of comparing their qualifications is needed. A current trend is to let several

CAREER MANAGEMENT

persons participate in this comparison in order to eliminate personal bias (to the extent this is possible).

6. *Notice of offer or rejection.* This need only be a simple telephone call by the manager or a personnel specialist to communicate the decision and the reasons for it.

7. *Formal move procedure.* Some clear-cut rules on how a man completes one job and moves to another are needed. It is desirable to state a maximum time limit for the change and to point out the man's responsibilities to his present manager and the latter's responsibilities to him.

Periodic audit. All systems are subject to exceptions. But the promotion system of a firm is so subject to manipulation that it is especially important for its observance to be monitored or audited periodically. So important is it for employees to view the system as fair and its implementation honest that such audit reports should probably be made directly to the president or to the vice-president responsible for personnel.

The audit can be simple—a random sampling of several promotions at different levels in the company that notes how they were handled, how the individual was finally selected, how those rejected were handled, and so forth. A president can reinforce observance of policy by complimenting the manager who handles a matter well, while some serious discussion may be in order if corrective action seems necessary.

Appeal or recourse. When a man is refused a job he feels qualified to handle or if he feels he was never considered at all, he inevitably has a negative reaction. This makes him more receptive to outside offers or spurs him to search for another job. Some of this reaction can be dissipated if the individual knows he can state his feelings without personal penalty and a quiet investigation can be made if warranted. Since, in some cases, the last person he is willing to talk to is his boss, the appeal probably must be to a third party, outside his chain of command. A designated personnel specialist with access to top management is a logical person to seek in a large organization. An assigned member of the president's staff may be suitable in a small organization.

Business Information

Imparting business information is seldom considered an essential ingredient of career advancement. It should be. It may well be more important than training programs and career discussions. The individual in a firm who understands the business he is in, the strategy used, the market, and the competition or lack of it can do his own job more creatively and can contribute ideas upward that influence the work of his department. With such influence comes personal involvement, and his goals begin to shape themselves around the goals of the firm.

In the absence of such information and understanding, he must be guided by the direction and counsel of his manager to a far greater extent. This leaves him with fewer choices and possibly a lessened interest in the company.

To help impart business information in an interest-arousing fashion, such devices as summit meetings to plan important projects, meet key goals, or solve major problems broaden opportunities for involvement. Debates on issues where there are difficult choices of strategy to make and membership on task forces or study teams that can make recommendations on specified matters above and beyond the scope of the individual's own job lend further interest.

Career Shifts

If an employee considers the desirable role of management to be a facilitating one, management's major interest is one of self-preservation and continuity of its function. It wants to attract and keep men who will perform in an outstanding fashion.

Does this mean, then, that the president of a company should strive to hold every employee for his full career—hire a man from college and finally retire him at 60 or 65? By no means. In this mobile age, not only is it becoming less likely in most cases that a company can do this; it's also probable that it should not do so.

There is much to be gained from a fresh look at a situation and from an avoidance of inbreeding. The gain is both to the man and to the institution. So it is probable that a man should be encouraged to seek a change of pace or position or firm at certain points in his career. If such moves are temporary, the organization must find a way to give the employee some options concerning his accruing benefits so that neither the firm nor the man is penalized economically.

Following are some suggested career shifts that might well be encouraged.

Back to school. This is especially important for specialists in areas of rapidly changing technology. A complete break with the firm, a relinquishing of one's job and devotion of full time to study is likely to be more rewarding than night school, part-time courses and the like. Most specialists need to get away and rethink their field and their commitment to it. They need enough time to be thoroughly refreshed mentally, emotionally, and physically.

Government or other nonprofit position. An exchange program might well be worked out to give some employees in the nonprofit sector of the economy an appreciation of the value of the profit motive, while permitting those in business and industry to understand the problems of government, hospitals and other nonprofit institutions. Each area has its advantages, each its frustrations. Much learning and improvement to both participants might result from such an exchange.

Teaching. For managers going stale on their jobs, a stint at teaching in a high school, junior college, vocational school, or college might be a real godsend toward bridging the generation gap, updating personal know-how, and becoming a better manager. Again, doing it full time for two to three years is more likely to pay dividends than teaching an evening course.

External consulting. The opportunity to sell one's services to other companies as well as to one's own employer may be especially desirable for specialists. It kills in-breeding and gives the individual an awareness of his personal value and the value of his specialized knowledge. It can help build favorable relationships with other companies, especially firms which can't afford specialization in depth and may not, in fact, need it for very long periods of time.

Contract employees. For employees who leave to seek other opportunities but who possess valuable know-how, there exists the opportunity to bring them back into the firm for specific short assignments on a contract basis. It may well be that this practice will increase in the future as career specialists choose their home ground and then offer their services to a number of employers rather than just one. The employee is then truly his own career manager and the firm buys his services on an as-needed basis.

Reevaluate Five- to Ten-Year Men

The employee need not be the sole initiator of career changes. If any employee has been on his job for longer than five to ten years, he might well be earmarked for a serious discussion about possible changes in responsibilities at a suitable time. Expensive? Probably not as expensive as letting him get stale so that creative work drops off dramatically, not only in his personal efforts but in those of others over whom he exerts considerable influence.

Outlined above are key aspects of management's role in facilitating careers. Next it is important to consider how, within this framework, the employee can be involved in the system to a far greater extent in the future than he has been in the past so that he can fulfill his personal career-managing responsibilities.

5

Equal Treatment of Employees and Applicants

A great executive in American industry once made a speech to the personnel department of his firm. "We ought to make it as easy for an employee to find a job in our company as it is for an applicant," he said. He was right. When an applicant goes into a placement office, he is presented with a list of open positions, told about the qualifications for each, and sent for a cordial visit with the manager who has the opening. He is encouraged to express his interests. He may be invited back a second or third time to explore further concerns. His wife may also visit the prospective employer, who answers her questions and discusses her interests. Finally, an offer is made. Sometimes several are extended and the applicant is allowed to choose.

CAREER MANAGEMENT

Obstacles in the Promotion System

An employee is seldom treated as well as the applicant just described. Let's consider some typical cases.

"I Did It the Hard Way. Why Can't You?"

Philip X. is a man in his early 20s. He joined the firm 21 months ago as a production specialist. His work has been excellent. Two performance appraisals, one after six months and another a year later, indicate that he has dug into the work, has grasped it fully, and is establishing fine relationships with associates. He has already made a number of suggestions for improving his work, and several have been adopted with good results. His immediate manager indicates that he is an eventual candidate for a management position. This evaluation has been discussed with Philip.

When Philip joined the company, he was quite clear about his intentions. He stated that he wished a managerial position within two years. He was assured by the recruiter at his college campus that, while the time was short, it was not out of the question. Everything would depend on his work and early attitude on the job.

Now that he is within three months of his target date, Philip decides to investigate the situation to make sure that his interests are understood and that he will be considered for suitable openings. He goes to the personnel office, where he is told that before the matter can be investigated his boss must agree to the discussion and exploration of new opportunities. He goes back to his boss, explains what is in his mind, and asks for approval to talk to someone in the personnel department. His boss, who up to this time has been cordial, cooperative, and supportive in every way, suddenly displays a different attitude.

"Now, look here, Phil," he says, "you just haven't been around long enough to get promoted. Why, some of us worked for 10 years before we even thought of a better job. It took *me* 14 years to make supervisory rank. You're too impatient. Besides, it's policy not to consider anyone for promotion until he's been with us three years." "But if I have the qualifications, why can't I be considered?" asks Phil. To which his boss replies, "Well, you see, you don't have the qualifications. You're not mature enough. And besides, there are lots of others ahead of you."

Since Phil is young and capable, this answer is far from satisfying. His reaction is likely to be one of disillusionment with the company followed by a decision to look elsewhere. Even if the job market is unfavorable, his attitude toward the company, the personnel department, and his boss has suffered a setback, and his dedication to the interests of the firm is likely to follow suit unless something unusual happens to regain his goodwill.

What little loss there would have been—and in fact how great the attitudinal gain might have been—if Phil had been free to have his discussion with the personnel man to register his interests and explore whatever openings might have existed. Had he gotten a better job, his loyalty and commitment to the organization would have increased. A replacement would have been needed, but certainly the timing of the move would have been negotiable. If he had not been offered a position, at least he would have known he was being considered, and he would have seen more clearly what he needed to learn in order to succeed next time. What's more, the manager might still have a well-motivated man on his staff.

CAREER MANAGEMENT

There's Never a Good Time to Move

Carl F. is a district sales manager in his late 40s. He has been in his job for some 10 years, and he realizes he's going stale. Carl knows his way around the company, so he goes to his boss and tells him how he feels and that he'd like to look at some other jobs. Does the following reply sound familiar?

"Carl, why do you have to pick a time like this? You know what we're up against right now. The president himself has said, 'Push product X,' and you know our region is way behind its quota. If you'll just see us through these next six months, we'll talk about it again. Besides, whom do you have coming along to take your place if you walk out right now? Don't you think you owe us some warning?"

The first time Carl hears that speech, he probably takes it at face value. But when some emergency prevents his try for a new opportunity time after time the story begins to wear thin. There are legitimate emergencies, of course, and people can be quite indispensable for short periods of time. But from the point of view of some managers, there is never a good time to change or move men, and there's always some insuperable barrier to replacement. The odds favor Carl's remaining in his job and growing increasingly stale in his work. It is hoped that he will seek greater satisfaction and development off the job. But the situation represents a needless diversion of his energies from corporate objectives.

Why should one man have so much control over the growth and advancement of another? All interests suffer as a result of it. Carl's working career plateaus at what may be an unnecessarily early stage, his work does not receive the imaginative effort it deserves, the firm loses some of its investment in Carl's potential, and Carl's boss misses an important experience in managerial development. Carl may of course seek an outside position, thus saving his career, but the firm then loses even more dramatically.

Freeing the Man for Promotion—or Abandoning Him?

Harry P. is 55 years old. He has come up the management ladder a considerable distance but feels he could take on more responsibility. His boss says he is willing for Harry to see what he can find, so he "makes Harry available." This means he sends a note to the personnel office saying, "Harry is a good man. He would like more responsibility, and I believe he can handle it. Please help him find another job. In the meantime, please send me applicants to replace Harry so that I am not caught short." On the surface, all this sounds reasonable. But as Harry goes for interviews, he finds that almost everyone says he's looking for a younger man with somewhat different qualifications. His manager, meanwhile, interviews a number of candidates, and the day inevitably arrives when he finds a suitable person to replace Harry. Now what happens? Harry finds himself forced to say whether he's going to stay or leave. He gets the impression that he had better go. If he is fortunate enough to have an offer at all, he feels he should accept it whether or not it seems better to him than the job he's leaving. He regrets requesting permission to look around and may indeed end up worse off than he was at the beginning.

This issue presents the other side of the managerial control coin. Abandoning an employee, cutting him loose, forcing him into a position of no return is almost as bad as refusing him any freedom at all. Any promotion or career system needs to avoid both extremes.

These examples portray three of the greatest managerial errors in establishing promotion guidelines: enforcing administrative rules (based on precedent and past career patterns) that may prevent the most capable men from being considered for advancement; controlling all employee actions to seek new positions within the same firm; and granting the employee permission to explore for new jobs without supportive action and then cutting him off from his old position.

Opening Up the Promotion System

What changes might be made to prevent these unfortunate occurrences? Let's move step by step through the typical promotion operation and suggest ways of both personalizing the system and opening it more to the employee's self-directive efforts.

Career Advancement Rather than Promotion

In most companies, promotion systems are administered by the personnel department. The first step toward a stronger system would be to modify or enlarge the definition of promotion to include the concept of career advancement.

In the typical promotion system, when an opening occurs the manager of the job writes up a set of qualifications for the personnel department, which then begins the screening process. Usually, the first candidate sort is by salary. The computer (or whatever system is used) presents a list of names of people whose salaries fall about 20 percent below the range of the open job. The next sort is for people within this list who have held their present jobs about two years. Finally, man specifications are considered.

But the arbitrary salary and tenure screenings have no

Equal Treatment of Employees and Applicants

doubt already eliminated some eligible candidates whose careers would be advanced by this position, even though their salaries would not benefit. Very bright, capable younger people are similarly denied consideration, not because they lack qualification, but because they are young, their salaries are too low, or they haven't been in their positions long enough.

Real progress can be made by minimizing the effect of the two arbitrary data-sorting steps and instituting practices that pinpoint individuals who, together with the firm, might benefit from the experience of this open position. Three such procedures might be called *standing permission for job seeking, future job targeting,* and *fifth-anniversary personnel scanning.*

Standing permission for job seeking. This means that every employee is given the privilege of visiting the personnel staff (or some other designated administrator) to discuss his career interests or to explore available opportunities without his immediate manager's permission. As soon as he indicates that he wishes to be considered a serious candidate for a position, he informs his manager so that the prospective and present supervisors can discuss his qualifications. If the employee avails himself of this standing permission, he assumes the responsibility for ensuring that his assigned work does not suffer during the process. If he is offered the new position, the timing of the transfer must of course be negotiated between the two managers.

Future job targeting. Under this procedure, the personnel specialist considers where the open job might lead if the incumbent were successful. Usually, there will be several future possibilities. Once he has determined them, he identifies people who have expressed an interest in these or similar jobs and adds their names to the candidate list, regardless of their present salary. Suppose a job as program manager starting at $15,000 opens in a defense company. In the past, successful completion of a stint as program manager has led to project manager or administrative manager responsibility. An astute specialist pulls the names and personnel files of all employees who have expressed an interest in either of these two jobs. He lets them know they are being considered for program manager, though it may be a horizontal move or even a demotion in some cases and a very big increase in others. Then he lets them decide whether or not they'd like to compete for the job.

Fifth-anniversary personnel scanning. This practice has the personnel specialist add to the candidate pool the names of all employees who have held their current jobs for five years or more, who have remained in approximately the same salary grade, and are now doing (or have in the past done) work related to the open job. He discusses with them the problem of getting stale in one's work and the need for new ventures to keep alert and on the move. He asks whether they wish to be considered for the opening as part of their plan to avoid obsolescence.

These procedures can eloquently express an organization's interest in an employee and effectively support whatever career plans he has for himself.

Breaking Set Patterns in Job Families

The second traditional screening practice is to scrutinize people currently in positions that are purported to prepare them for an opening. This step relies on the job-family con-

Equal Treatment of Employees and Applicants

cept, based largely on precedent. As employees advance within a company, certain job routes are traveled more frequently than others. These are labeled job families. Another use of the job-family concept is to study the qualifications for all positions, searching for common requirements clustered in certain areas of knowledge and skill that increase by degree or amount. At worst, this perpetuates the sins of the past and can lead up an increasingly specialized job chain.

A worthwhile method for developing job families creatively is to put all the jobs of a given organization on the table at a managerial training session and ask participants to find ways of building new families according to whatever criteria seem sensible to them, considering the requirements of top jobs in the organization. In most cases, a meandering or zigzag path with shorter tenure per job would be more satisfying and motivating to the employee and more rewarding to the firm than the present vertical routes. In any event, asking managers to find a number of different job families helps them break set so that they are more willing to consider people who present themselves as candidates from positions that are not traditional antecedents to the opening. It also helps the personnel office to step out of its ruts and view jobs from different perspectives.

This is not to imply that a fast in and out is desirable for all men in all positions but rather that in the early stages of a career, say, the first 12 to 15 years, wider exposure will pay handsome dividends in developing people, in enlarging the number of ultimate career choices open to them, and in giving a firm a larger pool of qualified candidates for top positions. This kind of diversity during the early career period will minimize penalties to all parties concerned. In later career stages, both the risk and the penalty for too rapid movement are high. Customers want senior management continuity, and top managers need time to live with and sometimes correct the unfortunate results of major decisions they have made.

Job Posting

After the candidate pool has been assembled, the next step is usually for a personnel specialist to examine the files of candidates, scrutinize appraisals of their performance, talk to their current managers, and finally prepare a list of the 5 to 10 most promising persons. Those who have done this task are aware of the petty, invalid factors that sometimes preclude the listing of some employees. If for example a manager is out of the country, no one will approve a candidate in his absence. Another man is rejected because of a note of hesitation in his boss's voice as he describes his qualifications. Still another person is dropped from the list because his manager assures the personnel office a promotion is imminent within his own department.

Assembling the candidate pool provides a unique opportunity to give employees access to the system. A simple device—job posting—will do it. This calls for posting in a predetermined place a brief description of the open position, the assumed qualifications of incumbents, the salary attached to the work, and a request for those who feel themselves qualified to apply in a specified fashion.

This system has enormous advantages. It says to every employee, "We want you to know about our openings and their requirements so that you can get yourself ready. We are open-minded about candidates. We want to be certain no one is overlooked." It would be impossible to buy the kind of favorable reaction employees have to such an attitude. Furthermore, it forces a manager to think through realistic requirements for the job in question. He would feel foolish indeed

Equal Treatment of Employees and Applicants

if his published notice didn't make sense. At the same time, it truly allows the employee to function as his own career manager. It helps him to review the current state of his experience, the direction in which he wants to move, and the nature of a good potential position while he evaluates both the work and monetary value of the posted opening. Job posting thus gives the employee personal involvement in the organization's career advancement process and a share in the responsibility for its successful operation.

To the administrator or personnel director, the disadvantages may loom large. He foresees that he will be forced to interview and otherwise investigate a large number of unqualified people and turn them down. This is time-consuming, delicate work and risks upsetting some employees if they are not pleased with the reasons given for their rejection. This means increased effort and expense for management.

These problems are temporary. When the system is first introduced, employees, especially overly confident candidates, naturally want to test it. After that, they display quite good judgment, and few unsuitable applicants come forward. There is indeed some extra work, but the advantages make it worthwhile. Frequently, it brings employees who had been overlooked to the attention of placement people. Records are updated to show completed course work, outside activities, and other matters that may influence future placement decisions. Hidden grievances are brought to light where they can be resolved, and improper management tactics are revealed in time for appropriate action to be taken.

There are some legitimate problems. A manager may wish to initiate a quiet search because he has decided that the incumbent is not working out but does not wish to hurt him by advertising the fact. Job posting here may need to be delayed or disguised, or the incumbent may have to be given

CAREER MANAGEMENT

a temporary assignment. But these situations are likely to occur in a minority of cases.

Peer Nomination

A procedure that works well with job posting is peer nomination for posted positions. Some capable individuals underrate themselves or for some other reason hesitate to declare themselves in competition for an opening. It's possible and in many cases desirable to encourage any employee learning of an opening to suggest the name of an associate or former manager he thinks is qualified for consideration. It's useful to ask the nominator to give the reasons for his choice and to supply his name if he is willing to be contacted for further information.

Since peer nomination adds to the administrative burden, an organization may want to initiate job posting first and add nomination by associates later.

Career Clinics

One of the clear advantages of a job-posting system is that employees begin to learn more about job requirements. Another underutilized device for putting the employee in the picture is the career clinic. Many colleges offer such a service to their students. They invite successful representatives of a number of professions to come to the campus and describe their work and what it takes to do it. This is of course intended to help students identify programs on which to concentrate their efforts as well as select career paths that fit their interests and life values. The same sort of program would be of great benefit within the business and industrial world.

Successful managers and specialists who are in the 5- to

Equal Treatment of Employees and Applicants

10-year stage of their careers might address employees in the 2- to 3-year range, describing what they do in some detail along with the advantages and disadvantages of their chosen specialty. In this way, they might help the relative beginners to see some of the next reasonable steps available to them. They can talk to groups, answer questions, and arrange for individual discussions with those who evince considerable interest. At this point in a man's career, such a clinic has substantially more meaning than it did in college, and it's quite possible that mutual exposure of these two groups may broaden both, giving the junior men some additional sponsorship and preventing the seniors from making selections only from among those already in their own part of the organization.

The career clinic idea might well be repeated on at least one higher level—the interested 5-year men with successful 10- to 12-year people.

Quinquennial Job Rotation

Some years ago, the most frequent method for bringing a young man into a firm was to place him in a rotation program for a period of time, usually lasting from six months to two years. While this is still used to some extent, the practice has lessened somewhat in recent years. Young college graduates have developed their technical competence to a high degree, and they're eager to settle into a job and use it. Many are newly married and anxious to stay in one place, either to start a family or to enable their wives to begin their careers. Perhaps job rotation options should be available at about the five-year point. Here's why.

After five years or so—and the number is flexible—a man begins to know his own capabilities a little better. He also becomes familiar with the nature of opportunities in the firm. He's more certain about what sacrifices he is willing to make for his career. Consequently, he often reopens the question of what he wants to do with his working life. If at this point a rotation program were open to him, it might present an ideal way to explore some alternatives and try his talents in somewhat different environments and under other managers. It would open new job opportunities for him, perhaps give him new sponsorship, and in general help him embark on the second stage of his career with more enthusiasm and confidence.

At first examination of this procedure, the administrative burden may seem large. While it is not insignificant, it is not so great as it may seem. Not all employees will take advantage of the program. Some will be deeply involved in jobs with which they are quite happy. Others will not want to take the risk of giving up a reasonable situation for an unknown one. Still others will have decided that they will reach their personal objectives through their present positions. These eliminations make the program workable.

Men and assignments must be selected carefully, suitable compensation arrangements need to be developed, and there must be advance agreement on how long a program can be sustained economically. Since the men are experienced, they should be easier to place on completion of the program than are new, young people. There would certainly be administrative costs. But companies are on the lookout for attractive new benefits to offer management and professional employees, and this program is certainly attractive to the man seeking career alternatives, yet relatively low in cost. For the firm, broadening the experience of employees through rotating assignments adds substantially to the candidate pool for higher-level positions.

Equal Treatment of Employees and Applicants

Selecting the Candidate

Adding devices such as job posting, career clinics, and advanced rotation programs to the traditional personnel office methods of choosing nominees should enlarge the pool of candidates from which to make a selection. It should also manifestly open opportunities to more employees. The next step in the promotion process usually consists of comparative interviews of candidates followed by the final decision and offer.

Normally, a manager sees each of the top candidates individually, interviews him, checks out his performance with previous managers, and finally narrows his choice to one or two people. He then proceeds to offer the job to them in the order of his preference. It seems unlikely to be coincidental that most choices are usually men who have worked for the manager in the past or are already within his own department. Administrative directives insisting that candidate slates include individuals from outside the company or department often produce only rationalizations that the man who already knows the organization is best qualified. To overcome this kind of thinking, something dramatic needs to be done to stimulate a more objective comparison of qualifications.

Some of the group problem-solving games used in the Assessment Center approach to selection and development are well worth considering.[1] One way to make use of these processes begins with the individual reviews as before. Then the leading candidates are asked to meet on a given date at a given place to engage in simulations or business games. The conditions vary so that during one exercise, candidates operate within assigned roles, and during another, they must select

[1] See Robert B. Finckle and William S. Jones, *Assessing Corporate Talent* (New York: Wiley-Interscience, a Division of John Wiley & Sons Inc., 1970).

roles for themselves; on one occasion, they are given tight time schedules, whereas on another, the issue might be one of creative or ingenious thinking with time pressures quite relaxed. The variations that can be used are many and can be selected to draw out the kinds of behavior demanded by the job. A member of the personnel office, the hiring manager, perhaps the incumbent of the open job, and the manager's manager should observe the exercise. What does each man contribute? Do the candidates exhibit different characteristics under these conditions from those they did in the interview? Such comparisons help broaden the basis on which promotion decisions are made.

There are some obvious objections to this suggestion. It may be difficult to find a convenient time for candidates to get together. It extends the decision-making period. Some candidates will object to the obvious competition. All true. But many hopefuls will welcome the chance to prove themselves, and the improved result can be worth the inconvenience and expense. Candidates who object can always be told the reasons for the practice, and if they do not wish to participate, they can remain under consideration, recognizing that part of their qualifications picture will be missing.

Notification of the Decision

The last step is to notify unsuccessful candidates. If an employee is already a member of the firm, he deserves a little more than the usual refusal letter or phone call. A productive alternative would be to offer each unsuccessful candidate who reached the final stage a career discussion with the hiring manager and a professional career counselor about why he was not selected. Even more important, they might review what appears to be a likely next job for him and some things he might do to get ready for it—courses, outside activities, work assignments, special projects, and the like. If the employee wishes, his current manager might also be a party to this meeting. The reason for including the professional counselor, of course, is to prevent the exchange of meaningless generalities and evasive replies and to fix on some specific development and career plans.

Expensive? Yes. But again, not so expensive as it may appear. Not all unsuccessful candidates will want or request such a session. The number of discussions can also be limited administratively to, say, one per year per man. The advantages? The man's awareness of the firm's interest in him is increased. At the same time, his prerogatives as manager of his own career remain intact. The meeting is for him, and he takes the lead in asking questions and ultimately deciding what he will do about the suggestions made to him. Finally, the manager filling the open job who knows such sessions may be held probably makes his decision with greater care. He becomes better trained in selection since he must collect and weigh his evidence in a way that will stand up under the scrutiny of others. This in itself may be worth the monetary investment. As a possible by-product, the rejected candidate may handle himself well enough in the postdecision discussion to impress the manager so favorably that he is remembered and sought after next time an opening occurs.

In summary, then, to give the employee access to a firm's promotion process, it is recommended that employees have standing permission to discuss career interests with members of the personnel staff and to explore job opportunities without specific approval of their immediate managers. It is further recommended that the names of those who have expressed interest in a position toward which a given opening leads and those doing related work who have been in their jobs for five years or more be added for consideration.

In the early career stages, it is suggested that more frequent horizontal moves be used to advance careers rather than the more typical vertical job-family route. Career clinics can help employees learn more about job requirements and challenges, and rotation programs at the five-year point to broaden their interests and capabilities can be helpful.

When an opening occurs, job posting is recommended so that interested employees may nominate themselves. As an aid to selection, group problem-solving business games among leading candidates will give managers added information on personal behavior and style. And finally, a professional counselor might work with the leading rejected candidates to help them develop realistic plans for themselves.

These suggestions for improving each step of the promotion process are offered in the hope that they will generate more creative ideas, so that not only are employees better able to manage their careers but institutions will find talent sooner, use it more fully, and thus reap the benefits of greater creativity and productivity.

A Fast Start for Young Employees

get to know people, and so on. Peter is doing what seems to him to be routine clerical work. Requests to buy certain items reach his desk. His job is to transcribe the request onto a standard order form. When information is omitted or unclear, he checks it out with the purchaser and elaborates on the form. Then he takes the order to one of the senior buyers, who tells him whether it is to be sent out for bids or should be placed immediately with a designated supplier. All the people in the department are so busy they barely have time to glance at the order and give him rapid instructions.

Peter does this work for about three weeks and finds it appallingly dull. He makes one attempt to change matters. He goes to his boss to suggest that the purchaser use the order form in the first place and that the department stenographer screen it for completeness and send it on its way. His boss is horrified. He assures Peter that it would never be properly done that way and that Peter just doesn't understand the situation. "Someday, when I have a little time, I'll explain it all to you." That day never comes. Peter checks with one or two longer-term young employees and is told that he is really serving an apprenticeship. If he'll be patient, he'll be given more responsibility in time.

But Peter isn't patient. He can complete his work in about half his working hours. He begins coming in late in the mornings and taking longer lunch breaks. He starts wandering around talking to people to find out what they do. After four months, his boss holds an appraisal discussion with him. Peter finds he is considered to be uninterested, not very hard working, given to socializing on the job, and exhibiting poor work habits. When he protests the unfairness of the evaluation, his boss retorts that he has failed to say that Peter is also argumentative and doesn't accept criticism very well.

An exaggeration? Not at all. The only exaggeration may

be that the appraisal was made and discussed after Peter had been with the firm only four months. In most cases the evaluation probably is only in the manager's head, but it is nonetheless used against the employee for a long time. It takes extraordinary perseverance and skill on the employee's part or a great deal of interest and help from senior men to extricate a beginner from such a situation.

Initial jobs and work assignments should be screened and monitored with as much care as prospective employees are given in the first place. This responsibility should be handled by a personnel specialist or a senior employee who has displayed an interest in young workers. Following are 10 rules to guide the monitor.

1. *Use the employee's training.* Make sure the actual work assignments utilize his training immediately. His skills are at their peak. They need application to secure them and to reinforce his understanding. Thus, the organization gets its money's worth, too.

2. *Focus on results.* Give him assignments that produce whole results, if possible, rather than having him carry out one part of a process or perform some activity both started and finished elsewhere. In this way, the man has some latitude for exercising judgment right from the beginning, and the firm gets a picture of the quality of that judgment and a better measure of his ability to get results.

3. *Assign him to a team.* If a unique problem cannot be assigned because its magnitude is so great that the efforts of several people are required, put the man on a team so that he is in on plans discussions, sees the work flow, and understands the results needed. He thus can do his part intelligently, will learn from associates, and will get a glimpse of what a working relationship really means.

4. *Make assignments short.* Make initial assignments rela-

tively short-term, perhaps no longer than a month; two weeks may be even better. Make sure he knows there's an expected completion date, why that date is important, and what other work hinges on it. This gives him a bogey to shoot for and teaches him about commitment to deadlines.

   5. *Request a work plan.* Even if the assignment is for only two weeks, ask for an informal, penciled plan of just how he intends to tackle the job and how much can be finished at various intervals. In this way, he begins to understand how planning contributes to work accomplishment, and his manager can discuss the approach and counsel him on it before he begins rather than subjecting him to possible exhortation and recrimination later.

   6. *Use measurement.* During the first few months, hold an informal review at his desk at each scheduled milestone. Congratulate him if he's on or ahead of schedule. Show him how to adjust his planning if he's behind. Work with him on ways to make up lost time that don't necessarily involve greater effort but that perhaps enlist the help of others or that use an easier or better method. In doing this, you help him see the value of measurement as an adjusting tool.

   7. *Enlist the contributions of others.* Include items in the assignment that need data or material from others. Make sure the employee doesn't try to do it all himself, thus proverbially reinventing the wheel, but rather urge him to seek the data or other requirements from others. This helps him learn how to enlist help from others with both the frustrations and the gains attendant on it.

   8. *Set priorities.* Once the employee has overcome the initial hurdles of working life, assign two or three projects at once all of which must be kept going. He probably needs to learn how to handle several things at one time, and he surely needs to learn about setting priorities. He no doubt

also needs emphasis on laying out the steps to achieve a result so that those taking the longest are scheduled to start earlier, thus forcing him to juggle some priorities that may not have been otherwise apparent on a day-to-day basis.

9. *Keep responsibility in his hands.* In counseling the beginner on plans and reviewing his progress at intervals, don't take over his responsibility. Offer suggestions, mention other people who might have useful experience for him to draw on, and propose alternatives if necessary, but leave the ultimate decision making in his hands. He may make some early mistakes. But if he must live with them and, it is hoped, rescue the situation, he will learn and grow from them.

10. *Give rewards and recognition.* When he completes a piece of work satisfactorily, be sure he knows that his contribution is recognized. Have him present his results at a staff meeting. Perhaps your boss might be informed so that he can say a congratulatory word. If the result is unsatisfactory, this is the occasion to explore the reasons for what happened and what might be done next time to avoid the same mistakes and improve matters.

Finding Men Who Make Good First Bosses

Just as parents' attitudes and behavior are important to a child in his early years, so a first boss is critical in forming the working attitudes and habits of inexperienced young employees. For this reason, it is important to screen managers to whom young college graduates are assigned as carefully as the graduate himself. The individual assigned the monitoring responsibility might do the following things.

1. *Get ratings on former managers.* Talk to young college

graduates who have been promoted or have gone on to new assignments. What were their first managers like? Check especially on how their bosses shared business information, what kinds of work were delegated, the amount of freedom and responsibility they felt they had, and any responses they received.

2. *Get ratings on present "first" managers.* Talk to college graduates who are still on their first jobs or who have left the company voluntarily or involuntarily. Check out the same issues.

3. *Interview new college graduate employees.* As each recent graduate is hired, sit down with him after his first month to discuss the management he is experiencing. Spot-check the work assignments of at least a representative sample.

4. *Attend staff meetings of first-level managers.* If the organization is large, get selected personnel specialists to help you cover staff meetings of lower-level managers to find out first hand about the information-giving skills of managers at the bottom of the organization structure.

5. *Obtain assessments from higher-level managers.* Request an evaluation of the abilities of first-line managers to orient and develop new college graduates as part of their overall appraisals.

6. *Obtain job evaluations.* As new college graduates move from their first positions to ones of greater or different responsibility, ask them to complete a brief evaluation of the work they have been doing. Did it use their knowledge and skill? Did it challenge them? Did it teach them about the methods and systems of the organization? Did it provide a way for them to form working relationships with others in the firm besides their immediate work group?

7. *Build a preferred list.* From this information, begin to build a list of suitable first supervisors or managers. Use this

list when placing new employees in first assignments. For most of them, it will insure a good opportunity for a fair start.

There is no reason these steps should be taken in secrecy. The whole question of which managers should serve as first bosses might well be analyzed at a managerial meeting. At the same time, the action plan can be exposed for discussion and suggestions. Make it clear, of course, that the inability of a given manager to work with and develop young people is not a reflection on his total managerial talents. It may be that the work he guides is inappropriate for a beginner, the timing is poor, or his temperament is more suited to older employees. Managers could be encouraged to suggest or withdraw themselves as suitable for the assignment.

In many organizations, it is already pretty well known who the good first bosses are. It has probably not seemed too important to highlight the fact. The suggestion here is to make this evaluation explicit so that those who appear suitable can be given special training in packaging and delegating work, encouraging personal responsibility, providing for adequate freedom of judgment, dealing with confrontations, and furnishing feedback. They will then be in an even better position to cope with the young college graduate and help him adjust to the working situation so that he'll be stimulated by it and grow from it.

Testing Reality to Learn About the Work World

Young people who take their first professional jobs are often entering a whole new world. Their idea of what it takes to be successful may have been formed by the offhand comments of a parent or other relative. Or they may have built up an image from books, movies, or television. The transition from academia to working life is a process that changes this imagined, preconceived idea of how one should act and react in a work situation into reality. The young person accomplishes this by acting as he believes he should and then observing the reactions of others along with the result or degree of success it achieves. If the reaction is not quite as he anticipated, he makes some shift or change in behavior and repeats the process. He also watches others around him for behaviors and attitudes he too might adopt. Some of this process is conscious; some is not.

This learning by trial and error and retrial is reality testing. All of us do it to a certain extent when we enter a new situation. With more mature people who have experienced similar situations before, the advance estimate is likely to be better and the swings in behavior more moderate. The young person, however, acting on less knowledge and perhaps with less fear of consequences, may display rather dramatic changes that startle the unaware manager. One example will illustrate.

Henry J. is a new engineering graduate. He is hired by a development organization to do testing for more senior men.

After his first day or two, Henry notices that the technical staff seldom arrives on time. So he begins to come late each day, too, much to his manager's chagrin. Henry has two shop people and a lab assistant involved in the tests to whom he gives technical direction. Since they are paid on an hourly basis, they must be there on time in order to be paid in full, and Henry is often needed to get them started on the day's work. What should Henry's manager do? The obvious. He should call Henry aside as soon as he notices his late arrival time and explain why his presence is needed at the beginning of the work day and why the senior technical staff has more freedom. There is no reason to believe that Henry will not alter his arrival habits as soon as he understands the situation.

This is a simple disciplinary situation. Other kinds of behavior may be more complicated and the manager's immediate, simple, factual explanation for requesting change even more necessary.

What should managers do when new employees test the limits of the work situation? They ought to encourage it, first of all, since this experimentation is good in that it shortens the orientation period. Second, they should recognize it for what it is and should not be dismayed or discouraged by the trials. If these are successful and help the employee get better results or get them faster, his manager should tell him so and why they work. If they're awkward or poorly conceived and impair his accomplishment, his boss ought to point this out and show why they're ineffective. If he can, he should suggest an alternative, though without making a great ceremony of the discussion. Simple, factual, rapid feedback with suggestions about what to do differently and why will do the trick.

Providing Reinforcement and Feedback

The manager's rapid reaction to an employee's reality testing serves, of course, to reinforce good performance and reflect the degree of success achieved. The need of the young person for such responses, frequent and specific, cannot be underestimated. The day-to-day interaction between a man and his first managers probably does more to shape his behavior and attitude than any other single experience.

There is, however, a need for a more formal session in which daily matters can be put into perspective and trends can be discussed and evaluated. Remember that the young graduate is used to very quick, frequent responses in the classroom. A question is posed; he answers or formulates an answer. In the ensuing discussion, he learns whether he was right or wrong. He is given quizzes at intervals and receives a grade and perhaps some comments. He writes papers and they, too, are graded and evaluated. Ultimately, there is a report card for the semester.

The work situation can be quite a contrast. The manager, insensitive to the need for response, may impart an occasional word of approval or frown of displeasure. A full year or more may pass before the specifics of what has been done well and badly are put on paper and a planned appraisal session is held. During this time, the young person goes through a period of considerable conflict. Some of his friends may be charging him with selling out to the establishment. He tries very hard to convince himself he has made a sound choice. Lacking sufficient feedback during this time and not really being sure how he is doing, he may literally be unable to resolve the conflict. This can impair his performance and impede his adjustment.

For these reasons especially, then, day-to-day interactions need to be supportive. At least by the end of the first three- or four-month work period, a formal appraisal of his work and those things that help or hinder its accomplishment should be made and discussed in some depth. It can be simple in content. How well has the man achieved results? What strengths has he already displayed? What one or two things might desirably be changed to improve work during the next six months? The discussion should be long enough to let the man talk fully and get his feelings and problems out on the table. If this kind of session is held at least two or three times during a man's first year of employment, it is probable that his adjustment time will be shorter, he'll feel more satisfied with his initial career choice, and his work output will improve.

CAREER MANAGEMENT

Tracking Attitudes of New Employees

Since the first two years are in many ways the most difficult for the young college graduate, his feelings during this time assume great importance. We know that the typical graduate expects a promotion by the end of his second or third year. Whether he receives it depends, as stated earlier, not only on his personal potential but on the capability he displays. This, in turn, depends on his assignments and on his manager's skill in delegating responsibility, giving information, and responding to his performance. Even though a manager takes steps to improve these skills, matters will seldom be perfect. So it is also wise to track employees' attitudes as they enter the firm and at intervals during the first two years.

An attitude survey administered by someone from the personnel office (or a senior administrator following the new graduates) is the simplest and probably most effective means of accomplishing this. The respondents should be allowed anonymity so they will answer fully and freely, although in large organizations the questionnaires can be coded to identify departments. See Exhibit 1 for a sample survey.

The results of such a survey will first of all pinpoint the manager or group of managers about whom employees are dissatisfied. Then administrators can step up manager training or hold face-to-face discussions with new employees to identify sources of concern, assignment changes that need to be made, or managers who should be taken off the list of men to whom new college graduates report.

Survey results may also indicate general concerns around which special communication programs, activities, discussion groups, and the like can be built. If the survey is taken every six months for the first two years, trends can be observed and either reinforced or countered by specific management actions.

Exhibit 1. New college graduate attitude survey.

In each question, circle the answer that most nearly applies.

1. *I make use of my training in my present job.*
   Fully.   Partially.   Very little.   Very little, but situation will change soon.

2. *I am able to use my judgment on how to do my work.*
   Fully.   Partially.   Very little.   Very little, but situation will change soon.

3. *I am responsible for obtaining a clear-cut result.*
   Fully.   Partially.   Very little.   Very little, but situation will change soon.

4. *I have the opportunity to work with knowledgeable associates.*
   Often.   Occasionally.   Seldom.   Seldom, but situation will change soon.

5. *My work has deadlines and I know what they are and why they were established.*
   Fully.   Partially.   Very little.   Very little, but situation will change soon.

6. *My boss expects me to put a plan in writing before I begin an assignment.*
   Often.   Occasionally.   Seldom.   Seldom, but situation will change soon.

CAREER MANAGEMENT

Exhibit 1, cont'd.

7. *My boss gives me the benefit of his experience so that I can use it in my work.*

    Often.   Occasionally.   Seldom.   Seldom, but situation will change soon.

8. *My boss takes note of good things I've done.*

    Often.   Occasionally.   Seldom.   Seldom, but situation will change soon.

9. *My boss tells me right away if he thinks I'm off the track.*

    Often.   Occasionally.   Seldom.   Seldom, but situation will change soon.

10. *I am encouraged to get help from other experienced people when I need it.*

    Fully.   Partially.   Very little.   Very little, but situation will change soon.

11. *When I have several things to do, I set priorities for the various jobs.*

    Usually.   Sometimes.   Seldom.   I have only one thing to do.

12. *In the last six months, I had a performance-appraisal discussion with my boss.*

    Yes.   No.   One coming up soon.

13. *My boss tells me about the business situation.*

    Fully.   Partially.   Very little.   Very little, but situation will change soon.

A Fast Start for Young Employees

Exhibit 1, cont'd.

14. *With respect to freedom on the job, I feel I have*
    Quite a bit.   Very little.
15. *With respect to asking questions of my boss, I feel*
    I can ask him anything.
    I must limit questions to work matters only.
    It is very hard to ask him questions.
16. *My boss is*
    Fair.   Unfair.   I'm not sure.
17. *On the whole, I feel this way about my job:*
    Pleased.   Somewhat unhappy.   Very unhappy.
18. *On the whole, I feel this way about the firm:*
    Pleased.   Somewhat unhappy.   Very unhappy.

Feel free to add any comments you may have that may not have been covered by the questions or that explain any of your answers.

Yet surveys are not enough. In small companies, the president or a vice-president should take the time to meet new college graduates individually or in small groups to tell them his personal views about the company and its mission, what he hopes for it in the future, and the obstacles it faces. Then he should ask for and listen to personal expressions of interest or doubt from the new employees.

In larger companies, a general manager, a plant manager, or distinguished members of their staff probably take on this responsibility. This practice dispels the faceless quality that some top executives have for the young and overcomes some of the fear of the generation gap that may exist on each side. Following is a sample agenda for such a meeting.

> **Agenda of Meeting Between Management and the New College Graduate**
>
> President's (or General Manager's) Introduction
>   What's the company's mission?
>   Why is the mission important to us?
>   What's the market like? Competition?
>   What's the state of health of the business?
> New Employee's Introduction of Himself
>   Personal background data
>   Why he joined this firm
>   Early reactions to job and company
>   Career interests
> President or General Manager Talks About Himself Briefly
>   His family, his personal interests, and his concerns
>   Career ambitions
>   Personal, meaningful experiences and what he has learned from them
>   Any disappointments and reasons for them
> What's Ahead
>   For the president
>   What he would like the company to achieve and the odds against doing it
>   What barriers lie ahead
>   What the special opportunities for this group are
>   For the new employee
>   What changes he'd like to see made
>   How he and his associates can contribute

Dealing with Confrontations

Students in the current college generation don't hesitate to express their opinions and values on most issues. They are

A Fast Start for Young Employees

skilled in confrontation tactics and use them if they disagree with those above or around them. Since most managers in business and industry grew up in quite a different atmosphere, one in which compromise was much more the order of the day, confrontation tactics often catch them off guard and make the managing role seem very difficult indeed. What can they do?

1. *Be prepared.* Expect your statements to be questioned by the young person. In fact, if he doesn't question them, ask him why not.

2. *Be pleased.* Yes. Think of it this way. The fact that he challenges your remark indicates his interest. If he didn't care, he wouldn't bother.

3. *Answer him when he asks "Why?"* Be so pleased when he asks "Why?" that you answer him, factually and in detail. Don't get emotional or defensive, though.

4. *If you can't or don't know the answer, tell him so.* You've lived with many a policy or practice so long that it's second nature. You may not have thought through the logic of it in a long time. If he attacks one of these matters, pause, think a moment or two, and then say matter-of-factly, "I guess I haven't really thought about this in a long time. I'll think about it tonight, see if it still seems sound to me, and talk about it with you tomorrow. Meanwhile, to be sure I consider your point of view, tell me how *you* feel about it."

5. *If he gets emotional, ask for a repeat.* If he gets carried away on a subject, hear him through—wait him out. Then either say, "I believe I understand your feeling. May I say it in my words and you tell me if I've got it straight?" And then do so. Or say, "I think I understand how you feel, but so I'll be certain, would you tell me once more?" Listen carefully, and then conclude with "Fine. I'll review the whole matter." You'll grow in stature and gain the respect of the

whole group by this handling, whereas an argument will buy you nothing.

After a confrontation, some resolution of differences is called for. If two positions are openly stated, explore together why each of you feels as he does. Then ask, "How can we resolve our differences enough to be able to work together effectively?" If some data-collecting task can be assigned to the employee that may help to resolve the dispute, that's usually productive. Don't be afraid to give in on small matters or to concede in some areas. Closed-mindedness is one of the marks of age. Don't yield to it. Save your holdout position for major issues, and even in these cases, try to understand the other side fully.

This, then, is the recipe for getting young college graduates off to a fast start. Strengthen the jobs they do (we should anyway; salaries are so much higher than they used to be). Screen managers (not everyone is a successful parent in dealing with the younger generation; why should all managers be expected to establish good working relationships?). Allow and encourage freedom to experiment but give immediate, clear, specific, and constructive feedback. Increase performance appraisal discussions to two or three during the first year. Track attitudes and bring top management and new graduates together for dialog. Be prepared to have policies and practices challenged, and welcome this as an opportunity to update and improve them. If these things had been done in your day, your own career might have moved along more swiftly.

7

Advancing Careers of Minority Professionals

WHEN the Civil Rights Act of 1964 was first passed, there was a drive to put members of minority groups on payrolls. By now, the extent of our success is clear. While the numbers have improved considerably in some cases, other problems have been created. Well-qualified blacks, for instance, were much sought after and could name their own price. They often changed jobs when a new employer outbid the present one.[1] Only the more mature and self-disciplined realized the importance of searching out a meaningful job in order to gain solid experience along with the opportunity to prove themselves and to enlarge their talents.

Now the frenetic competitive hiring has subsided some, and it's time to look at where we stand and how the next steps taken can be more meaningful. A clear goal is to find

[1] See John S. Morgan and Richard L. Van Dyke, *White-Collar Blacks* (AMA, 1970).

ways to offer promotion and advancement to minority employees. But before we can offer these, we must allow candidates the opportunity to earn consideration by demonstrating their capabilities. And in order to do this effectively, we have to overcome some of the management errors committed in the hiring race. We'll begin, therefore, by discussing the major mistakes and oversights displayed in personnel practices with minority employees of professional status. We'll also suggest some necessary actions to recoup lost ground and build stronger career foundations. On the mistake side of the ledger, we'll review the effects of overpricing, overprotection, tokenism, and showcase hiring. On the omission side, we'll discuss the dangers of inadequate or inaccurate responses, underdelegation, insufficient confidence, and arm's-length management. Finally, five recommendations will be made for effective career advancement of minority professionals.

Costly Errors in Minority Advancement

In discussing the mistakes made in the rush to comply with civil rights laws, we do not intend to criticize those who erred. Under the circumstances, certain mistakes were understandable, and in some cases there was no clear alternative. The purpose in examining them is to determine the likely effects on the victims—willing and unwilling—so that positive actions can be taken based on the reality of present situations.

Overpricing

Howard B., for example, is a qualified, capable engineering graduate of a predominantly Negro university. He is well trained; his grades were good; his personality is excellent. During his senior year, he found the opportunity to spend more time talking to industrial recruiters than in the classroom. Invitations to visit companies large and small, meet their executives, and discuss a variety of job opportunities were so numerous that he ended up with more than a dozen offers and might have had others if he had not stopped interviewing in order to get his studying done. All this was a pretty heady experience for Howard. He had confidence in himself and realized that most of the interest shown him was deserved. On the other hand, he was aware that at other times in history the situation would not have been quite so glamorous. As a result, he was torn between wanting to believe the interest was personal and based on his qualifications and the sneaking suspicion that the companies were playing the numbers game and had a different motive for wanting him in the firm. Regardless of the offer he finally accepted, Howard thus began his career under the pressure of self-doubt, which put him unnecessarily on the defensive.

Naturally, in making his selection, Howard accepted one of the better offers, balancing the money against the known characteristics of the firm he chose. He did, after all, want to work for an outfit with a good reputation and with senior technical staff from whom he could learn. It didn't take long for him to discover that he is receiving premium pay compared with that of other engineers at the entry level. This by itself doesn't concern him, but what he is asked to do is often less important and less demanding than some of his associates' assignments. This adds to his self-doubts and also undermines his confidence in his manager and in the firm. He tries to convince himself that he has made a wise choice. As his first year progresses, he finds that other companies continue to woo him. He receives new offers, some pretty tempting. If his personal concerns rise high enough, he may change jobs—perhaps more than once, should the situation repeat itself.

What are the effects on his career? The damage to his self-confidence, already mentioned, can be serious. If he remains with his first employer, salary increases may not come as rapidly as he has anticipated and their size may not match his expectations. For company management, at the same time, has to balance employee salaries on an equitable basis in terms of individual contribution. This will serve to reinforce his self-doubt and ambivalence about his position.

But if he changes jobs once or more, his learning will probably suffer, and the first two working years, which should be the time for establishing a career foundation, will not have filled this purpose.

Overprotection

A man could start at a higher salary than his associates with good, solid work assignments to support the added pay. In the case of a minority employee, however, the manager with good intentions may fail to give him difficult jobs for these reasons: "I don't want him to experience failure or antagonism, or to be hurt or to lose us business, or. . . ." But the learning experience of the early work years comes from testing one's wings to find out what can and can't be done. The best time to make mistakes is during the first year or two when they are not likely to be so costly for either the man or the firm. Thus the overprotective manager denies the minority employee some of the most important learning experiences of his life and in so doing undermines his career foundation.

The overprotection syndrome is most often seen in the sales function, where the black salesman may be restricted to minor customers and uncontroversial accounts. In some cases, managers have even called a customer to warn him that a black salesman was on his way. This denies the man the opportunity to test reality and thus learn the limits of the situation so that he can build his own method of operating that is suitable and effective.

The problem is dual. The manager is really trying to be helpful and the employee, a little nervous at the outset, may actually be grateful that not too much is asked of him. But the two are on a collision course. They're contriving an unreal world. Sooner or later, normal patterns recur, and the minority employee may not be equipped to deal with them so well as his less protected associates. The other extreme could be equally damaging—sending him to the toughest, least probable customers or putting him in impossible situations with little advance preparation. This has been done, too, so that the failure of the employee has been cold-bloodedly calculated.

But somewhere between the two extremes lies a course of action that leads the employee from simple situations to more and more difficult ones in which his manager provides full information beforehand, discusses possible tactics, and then gives him his full chance.

Tokenism

Some firms and some managers have felt it necessary to comply with the letter but not the spirit of the Civil Rights Act. They hire one black, one Mexican, or one Oriental as evidence of good faith and then argue that everything possible has been done to find qualified candidates but to little avail. This is tokenism, and it has an effect on the man hired. First of all, he knows or gradually becomes aware of his situation. If he is a serious professional, he feels used, and his inner confidence is certainly not helped.

More than this, the token minority employee finds himself in an impossible situation from a career viewpoint. He may find the atmosphere friendless and feel cut off from normal informal channels of communication. Even more important, he finds himself competing solely against Whitey, and this may be a ball game for which he is not prepared and for which the ground rules are not very clear. When several minority employees are hired, they can compare notes, exchange information, help each other, *and* compete against each other as well as against their white associates. Tokenism in the long run can only result in increased turnover among minority employees, which in turn reinforces the prejudiced manager's view that "These people are unreliable" and he doesn't want too many of them around.

Showcasing

The rather obvious placement of a minority employee in the employment office, the reception area, or some other showcase spot indicates that management is trying to prove to the world its lack of prejudice and discrimination. Merely placing people in such spots is not a particular hazard to their career growth; but it can be a signal that the system for implementing their advancement is not functioning. Moreover, the person placed in such a showcase position is often the object of a combination of tokenism and showcasing in that he has few qualifications for the work, little is expected of him, and indeed he has little to do but be there, displaying management's good intentions. This can be devastating to the employee. Whatever skills he has are soon lost and whatever confidence might have carried him through the transition period is rapidly undermined, to be replaced with bravado, rebellion, or withdrawal.

Costly Omissions in Minority Career Development

Such errors as overpricing, overprotection, tokenism, and showcasing are only one side of the coin. On the other are a number of serious management omissions that slow the employee's growth and hold down his level of performance. Let's look at several important ones.

Inadequate and Inaccurate Responses

In the preceding chapter, it was pointed out that young people need clear, substantive day-to-day reactions to their effective accomplishments and to those that need to be changed, and that they should be encouraged to experiment and test reality so that they begin to learn about themselves and how to function effectively in business. A minority employee entering the business world for the first time at any age needs these same kinds of information.

Unfortunately, because of cultural differences (or more likely because of fear of cultural differences), there is a certain uneasiness in the relationship between a minority employee and his manager. As a result, managers have been more delinquent than usual in performing this essential responsibility. If they are confronted with this charge, their rationalizations are fantastic. "Well, I have to give him a little time to adjust" is a frequent comment. But how will the man adjust if he doesn't realize that what he is doing or failing to do is not useful? Another says, "I don't want to hurt his feelings." Would anyone truly prefer to substitute a lifetime hurt for a few painful moments?

Even worse than no reaction is truly inaccurate feedback. Joe L., on his first accounting job, is making the usual mistakes of the new employee and is failing to submit all his reports on time. Does his manager tell him so? No. He slaps him on the back and tells him, "You're doing fine, Joe." How will Joe grow in these circumstances? How will the manager explain to Joe why he hasn't gotten a better job in a few years?

How often have you heard it said, "Yes, I know that work isn't being done right. We have a Puerto Rican [or Mexican-American or whatever ethnic background] in the job, and you know, we just can't fire him"? There is racism of the rankest sort.

The limiting effects of such treatment on the individual's growth and personal career management are so obvious they need no further elaboration.

Underdelegation

Delegation of trivia or work fragments is a serious managerial failure. Even managers who are normally good delegators sometimes fail with the minority employee. He is asked to do certain tasks but is not given a complete assignment to achieve. He may be given just enough information to carry out instructions but not enough to allow him to make any choices. And so his judgment, which is one of the essential ingredients in professional and management positions, is not developed. The supposedly successful employee operating under these conditions must be a robot. What is the effect on his career advancement? If he stays, he's limited; if he leaves, he starts over and probably must undergo an unlearning process. Sometimes the reason for underdelegation is the overprotectiveness of the manager. Sometimes it is lack of trust or of full communication. Whatever the reason, the result is the same.

Underconfidence

A manager's lack of confidence may show itself in a number of ways. Underdelegation is one. Another is his behavior in delegating work to a minority employee. He may assign the man a week-long project. Then he might come back in a day or so to ask whether work on it has started yet and if so what has been done. He may even go so far as to ask an associate of the employee's to look in on him to see whether he needs help. This kind of checking is bound to irritate the employee or make him nervous, depending on his feelings of security or self-confidence.

Attitudinal expressions of distrust may be more difficult to describe, but they're just as obvious to the employee. The manager's attitude is the sum and import of all the things he says or fails to say, the way he says them, his response and reaction to questions, his facial expression, gestures, and all the other verbal and nonverbal cues that convey the message, "I don't think you can do this or will do it or want to do it." Its effect on the employee's estimation of his own value can be devastating. He may refuse to do anything without the direct approval of his boss. He may spend an inordinate amount of time asking his associates how this or that is done to make sure he does it right. Or if he has strong confidence in his own abilities, he may turn rebellious, bent on belligerent win-lose confrontations. Or he may simply make a job change.

Arm's-Length Management

A good part of a happy business experience consists in the relationships, both working and social, that are built in the course of day-by-day work. These relationships find expression in frequent discussions among the parties who enjoy them. Not all the informal talk will be directly focused on work, although much of it is. And it serves to condition people in the organization for changes that are about to occur. For example, during an informal lunch, a manager tells others at the table about some of the ideas expressed by a new boss. He comments on his feelings about these ideas. Other members of the group may chime in and give theirs. Afterward, those who took part in the discussion are not surprised when some of the ideas come to fruition. They may find that their manager has quite unconsciously altered his views on the basis of their comments. All of this permits the total group to be prepared, to begin to incorporate some of these ideas in their actual work at a very early stage.

Think of minority employees in this framework. Some are drawn into the closely knit circle of relationships. Probably more are not, or at least they go through a somewhat longer transition period than usual during which they are not included. They do receive letters and reports that are sent to all. They do attend basic meetings to which others at their level are invited. The manager cannot be faulted for failure to include them in any of the regular, formal channels of communication. But in the informal bull sessions, the gossip, the exchanges that give color and life and advance notice of change, they are overlooked. As a result, there is an inevitable disadvantage, temporary though it may be, to their work performance, and to this extent their career launching is impeded.

Career Advancement for the Minority Professional

There are a number of problems, then, facing the minority employee who wishes to manage his career sensibly and soundly. These problems developed largely because of the rush to comply with civil rights requirements in a conspicuous fashion. What can be done to solve these problems over the short range and make it easier for the employee to add to his responsibilities and achieve his career goals? Five specific things are recommended.

Management by Objectives

Management by objectives (MBO) is advocated so much by management theorists today that it appears to be a sort of patent medicine. Although this is certainly not the case, at the present time it is surely a very important aid to minority career advancement.

Management by objectives, simply defined, means translating business plans of the firm down through the various levels of management to the point where each person whose work supports the basic plans has a set of related goals that he is trying to achieve within a given time period. His manager evaluates his success, then, in light of whether or not he is meeting these goals. The obvious advantages of such a process are that what is delegated is explicit, how it is measured is clear, and the individual knows as well as his manager whether he is achieving expected results. Thus, some of the errors described earlier can be corrected. The showcase job with its lack of substantive content cannot exist in an MBO system. The manager who delegates an activity or a small piece of work is forced, if MBO is used, to package the work in terms of results. If a manager habitually gives insufficient or inaccurate feedback, his inadequacies will be minimized since with clear targets and clear results the employee knows as well as his manager whether or not he's succeeding.

How does MBO help career advancement? Measurements protect minorities. It has frequently been pointed out that the reason black athletes were accepted so early and have been so successful in sports is that in the sports world the goals and measures are clear: a good batting average and a high score on home runs just cannot be overlooked.

In industry, a man is usually considered for a better job only when he has succeeded in his current assignment. If, then, we can make his accomplishments undeniable through the MBO process, the minority worker is in a far better position to be considered for promotion.

Confrontation on Cultural Differences

MBO suggests evaluating employees according to results, not personal likes and dislikes. But judgmental decisions are still made. Many of these, by managers' own admissions, derive from personality, relationships, attitude, and similar factors. The minority employee who comes from any other than a middle-class American family may not respond in group and individual situations the same way as the WASP—the typical white Anglo-Saxon Protestant. Managers whose values have been formed by association with WASPs may rate down something that is different though not necessarily poorer, thus creating further problems. To the minority employee, it looks like and of course it is prejudice. To the manager, it is not a conscious bias. He simply has not had broad enough experience to see the merits of other behavior patterns.

If the matter is left to smolder beneath the surface, little progress will be made in overcoming such ills as overprotection, underconfidence, and arm's-length management. Only the frank exchange of views, open confrontations of value differences, exploration of reasons for differences, and reconciliation or agreement to disagree will help solve the problem. This kind of process is best guided by professional group dynamicists or people skilled as catalysts in confrontation and resolution techniques. If everyone involved can achieve mutual understanding and at least some enlargement of his experience, the way to advancement for the supposedly different minority worker is going to be much easier.

Realistic Customer and Interpersonal Relationships

Even if a manager is willing to examine and test his values and enlarge them to include those of the minority worker, the employee must still face the reactions of others—of customers if he is in a contact position and of those within the company with whom he must do business in the course of doing his job. Protecting the employee so that he doesn't get a chance to learn how to handle these relationships is clearly unfair. "Treat me like a man. Give me the chance. How do you know I can't do it?" one young black salesman says. And that is certainly the first rule. Minorities have as much "right to fail," as it is sometimes called, as any WASP.

Perhaps the simplest thing to do is to say to the salesman, "Look, try again. If after several tries you conclude it's hopeless, tell me and we'll try another salesman. After all, every one of us meets some people who will not see us or won't do business with us. Sometimes the reasons are legitimate, sometimes not. So the main thing is not to hit your head against a stone wall but recognize the problem and devote your energies to other customers with whom the probability of payoff is higher. It's the results we need—the dollars and the sales volume. If you can't get it one place, get it another. We'll find some way to take care of the isolated guy here and there who judges our product by the way your hair is combed." This sort of plain language is usually acceptable. It will seem sensible to most and should clear the air and allow all involved to face matters realistically.

To help the employee handle internal contacts, invite those who frequently work with him to join the confrontation group if this is possible. If not, at least allow him to try to work matters out for himself. If a reasonable trial period shows no improvements, only then should the manager intervene.

More Career Information

It may be that the professional minority employee lacks a certain advantage open to his WASP counterpart, namely, an understanding of the rudiments of career paths. Quite often in the childhood home of a young WASP employee, much of the dinner-table conversation revolved around his father's experiences in the working world. Although the man's personal perception of his company probably dominated the anecdotes, nonetheless the boy acquired a sense of how things are done in business—how one gets ahead, what sorts of knowledge and skill seem to be required, and so forth. This kind of information may well be missing from the experience of the minority worker. Therefore, career clinics, described in Chapter 5, or any reasonable substitute should be offered. Clear information should be given both to groups and to individuals concerning business plans, how organizations function, what the organization structure is, what work makes up each job in the hierarchy, and the job requirements for higher-level positions to which a man might reasonably aspire.

Probably such sessions should be developed especially for minority workers. This is not to exclude others or deprive them of needed information but rather to insure that minority workers' questions are given full vent without fear of criticism from white associates.

Personal Career Models

Minority employees in key positions who have made it or are making it to the top are badly needed to serve as models for young beginners. One can usually find an exceptional individual who would have reached the top despite any handicap. But the typical minority employee, newly introduced to the business world, finds it hard to identify with a genius. He needs models in whom he sees something of himself—with some strengths, some weaknesses. The success of such models in the organization hierarchy gives him hope, an example he can trust, and some behavior patterns and work methods to copy. Such a successful person represents factual evidence that the company is really willing to give all competent people an opportunity. It thus encourages in the employee greater effort at career management, more confidence in himself, and greater pride in his origins. Organizations would, therefore, be well advised to recruit individuals who might serve as models. It is also probably wise to take more than the usual risks in promoting promising minority workers in an effort to provide this example for less senior employees.

8

Women and Career Opportunities

THE Women's Liberation Movement has brought to the forefront (not always in a way designed to stir the supportive imagination of the male tycoon) the pent-up feelings of women who seek or have sought careers in addition to or different from that of wife and mother. Although women are protected to some degree under Title VII of the Civil Rights Act, prejudice toward women differs from racial bias. Many of the remedies described in the preceding chapter apply to women (who are, after all, usually in the minority in professional and management ranks), but there are additional problems and solutions to be considered. As has been pointed out so many times in recent years, the conventional psychological and sociological images of women are challenged by current career emphases. In turn, the traditional male role is threatened. It's pretty hard to tell which is more disturbing to people.

In this chapter we shall not attempt to argue women's rights, the increasing level of knowledge among women, or the need for their potential contributions. Neither shall we compare women's mobility with that of men or comment on the investment risk women represent to most employers. Others have worked this ground thoroughly. Suffice it to say that with changing life styles, the decreasing birth rate, and the rise of male job mobility, the risk is equalizing. Instead, we make the assumption that organizations will abide by the law and increase the number of women hired into professional and management ranks. Given that assumption, we shall examine actions that management and women can take in turn to facilitate the latter's career advancement. Under management's responsibilities, we'll consider special positions, first jobs, short-term leadership assignments, the inclusion of women in management meetings, the importance of feedback on performance, and the need for career models.

As for ways women can help themselves, we'll discuss women working for other women, men working with women, men reporting to a woman manager, and ways a woman can overcome some of the special difficulties she faces in a managerial role.

The Facilitating Management Role

There are economic motives for putting effort into training the disadvantaged to do useful work: to reduce their dependence on welfare and increase their buying power. Although the numbers are not quite so compelling for advancing minority employees in the professional and management ranks, the argument is still partially valid.

In the case of women, however, the economic motive for

improving their status is in direct opposition to another powerful one. Women have traditionally filled certain kinds of jobs with great skill—as secretaries, office managers, administrative assistants. In these positions, they have been considered the right arm of many male executives. Such jobs still need to be filled. If the best female working talent in the nation is diverted upward into professional and management positions, a void will be left that will not be easy to fill. In addition, whereas women's salaries in these supporting positions have not come close to matching those of the male executives served, in most cases the salaries have been adequate to support the woman at a minimal level or supplement the family income. So the buying-power argument is only partly convincing, and there remain counterforces that limit wholehearted devotion to facilitating female career advancement. Certainly there have been and will continue to be exceptional women who make their way up to executive levels, but for the usual case, the Civil Rights Act as it applies to women needs the support of business through affirmative action plans to give its mandate thrust and make better opportunities a reality. Granting their existence, however, here are some specific suggestions for helping the typical educated woman who desires it to achieve professional and management stature.

Avoid Creating Special Positions

A device frequently used for upgrading capable women is to create special new jobs for them. On the surface, nothing appears wrong with this practice. The woman defines and develops the job using her unique combination of strengths, often making a sizable contribution.

The less obvious problem is that no comparison can be made of her productivity and skill with those of male counterparts, and thus, while her responsibilities may be heavy, her salary level is often solely a matter of managerial judgment. In addition, the career path is not nearly so clear since others have not passed this way on their way up the organization ladder. It's rather common for a woman to leave one of these special positions and be replaced by a man. Shortly thereafter, the salary level rises significantly, and the job finds its way into suitable job families.

The suggestion here is not to eliminate such special jobs, since they can be extraordinarily developmental and rewarding, but rather to place women more often in established positions formerly filled by men. This allows not only more proper compensation scales but direct performance comparison and therefore direct competition with the male performer, perhaps refuting the old saw that if a woman is given a job, twice as much is expected of her as of a man.

Make Her a Trainee, Not a Typist

Everyone has to start somewhere, and the beginning is often a breaking-in activity in which the employee functions at a level somewhat below that of his training. In earlier chapters, it was suggested that the time allotted to this be shortened and a person's professional training put to use sooner. In the case of women, this has special significance. Many professionally trained women are told in employment offices that the way to a better future is the clerical or secretarial route. This is nonsense. There is seldom a relationship between secretarial work and a desired profession. Moreover, while a woman is functioning at the clerical level, losing her professional know-how, she is also being trained implicitly not to take responsibility for her decisions. It's true that she may have considerable latitude in her job and may frequently use her judgment in her boss's absence. She is still, however, functioning in his name. He backs up her decisions, perhaps criticizing her for wrong ones but nonetheless taking the ultimate responsibility. Most women who have filled this role over a long period find the transition to self-reliance and personal decision making very difficult. They have learned to rely on the support of the boss's office. In face-to-face competition with associates, bosses, or even those lower in the organization, there lies a whole area of persuasive negotiation in which they have never had experience. This lack places them at a grave disadvantage. For these reasons, if professional work is the goal and the requisite training and skills are there, a woman should be started as would a man—in an intern or apprentice role, not with the typing and shorthand routine.

Assign Short-term Leadership Responsibility

If a woman's first job lays the technical groundwork adequately for higher-level professional work and management responsibility is her goal, additional ways must be found for her to develop leadership skills. Because working for a woman might have an unfavorable effect on male egos, certain devices may be needed to break down some traditional barriers. One suggestion is to give women short assignments as full- or part-time task-force leaders or committee chairmen. With the assignment kept short, she is able to try her wings in an area in which she may have had little experience. Disruption of work routines can be held to a minimum, and there is substantially less risk for both her and the organization than if she were placed in a full-time supervisory position in which she succeeds or fails.

The short-term nature of the assignment also protects the male ego. He knows this is an ad hoc group to be endured for, say, a couple of months. Moreover, he is not alone in this situation—he can share any embarrassment he may feel with other men. And the woman reaps substantial benefits. She gets practice, tries herself out in this role, and learns something about her own reactions to the situation and her own development needs.

Another suggestion involves a similar device. When a work overload occurs, once a woman has established herself in a given professional position, a man or two can be temporarily assigned to work with her on a loan basis until the hump is passed. Administratively, the men continue to report to their usual boss while helping out in an area of only passing needs. This again serves to protect their egos, provides them with the opportunity to find out what it is like to work for a woman, and gives the woman another way to test herself and develop her skills.

A third suggestion is to prohibit all-female units. Women who find it difficult to hire men for their workforces sometimes limit their appointments to women. This tends to isolate the unit and create a distorted perception of the work produced. It may peg the woman as a supervisor who is capable of managing only other women. Thus her career may inadvertently be limited, at least temporarily. Arbitrary edicts are seldom advocated, but this is one situation that might benefit from such a rule during the current social transitions.

Include Women in Summit Meetings

At one time or another, almost all organizations hold planning conferences or summit meetings. These sessions are usually highly interactive ones during which ideas about where the organization is going and how it might get there are freely exchanged. They often produce good preliminary plans and a strong feeling of unity among participants. It shouldn't have to be necessary to make a point of including women in these meetings. Since sometimes only one or two women are qualified to attend, however, they are often excluded on such archaic grounds as "There'll be a smoker one night and they won't fit." This can be so limiting to women's career progress that top management ought not only include those qualified but find certain roles that other women might fill at the meetings. These should be not merely secretarial or administrative, but rather some special work with direct bearing on organization plans on which a knowledgeable woman might report. Or a woman might be appointed to a special preplanning committee, attending the meeting in order to follow through on its initial efforts. Or she could chair a discussion group whose work she is especially interested in or qualified to lead. This sort of participation underwrites the professional woman's involvement in company- or organizationwide matters, begins to enlist her contribution on a different plane, improves her professional image, and prepares her directly for later managerial roles.

Respond with Adequate Feedback

The need for full, frank, rapid feedback exists for women as well as for other employee groups. The woman has a special problem, however. The typical male manager does not want to hurt her feelings. He may, in fact, be afraid she'll cry, so he avoids this serious responsibility. (Former female employees have of course helped condition him to feel this way, a point to be discussed later.) The issue here is that if feedback is too light, too severe, too general, or nonexistent, it misleads the woman, keeps her from making necessary adaptations and

Women and Career Opportunities

adjustments, and hampers her development in a most unfair fashion.

Of course, feedback to women, as for all other individuals, needs to be given with a helpful, supportive attitude if it is to be accepted and used. As in the case of minority employees, most women probably need more encouragement, more support, and more prodding to try new things and explore new areas. The career-woman image may not be well defined in the working woman's mind. She needs to develop it for herself. This means experimenting and testing reality, which she is likely to do only if her boss gives her positive encouragement and remains open in discussing the results of her probes.

Provide Career Models

Just like the male minority employee, the woman embarking on a career needs a model to look to, someone to emulate. A combination Cleopatra, Madame Curie, and Aimee Semple McPherson is not a particularly good one. Far better that she have a more typical woman, closer in age and obviously on her way up the ladder. It would probably be even more helpful if the progressing woman were married. The idea that a career woman must remain single, that a choice must be made between husband and work, has kept many qualified women out of the workforce except to take the most casual, short-lived jobs.

If a firm has a married couple, both professional, both working (perhaps not together but at least in the same company), it demonstrates far better than written words, persuasions, and exhortations that a happy marriage and a happy career can be worked out for both parties.

The suggestions given here imply that management should not merely permit these actions but rather go out of its way to effect them. Nothing recommended is expensive. Each activity requires only interest, positive attention, and relatively little effort to accomplish.

Career Management and Women's Responsibilities

The Woman Manager with Female Employees

Women employees often make life difficult for a female boss. A secretary may refuse to work for a woman. "She's too fussy. She expects too much. She works me too hard." These are fairly common complaints, and many secretaries do indeed wind their male bosses around their little finger. They use feminine wiles to get an extended lunch hour, an extra day off, time to do Christmas shopping, and so on. The woman moving ahead, not asking such concessions for herself, may be quite impatient with these tactics and much less sympathetic than her male counterpart. It would be easy to say that women must pull together to help one another. But these attitudes and reactions are deeply ingrained, and the likelihood of dislodging them by exhortation is pretty small.

Thus women are advised not to be dismayed by a negative attitude from clerks and secretaries. They should expect it, at least temporarily, and simply screen out those who would find it difficult to work for them. Happily, the more mature secretary is less likely to behave this way, and because of her maturity she'll probably be a better secretary. So the woman manager should allow a little more time for search, hiring temporary employees to fill in if needed while she looks for a suitable person. She might keep a list of women who appear capable so that she is not starting from zero when an opening occurs.

As for the professional woman working for a woman manager, she'll probably feel more comfortable with both men and women in the work unit.

Problems Men Have in Working with Women

Tears. "I talked to her about her performance appraisal and she burst into tears. I think I did everything right. I warned her in advance an appraisal was coming up. We set a time convenient to us both. I used my office; everything was private; there were no interruptions. I was just as gentle as I know how to be . . . and still she burst into tears. What an unnerving experience." These are one manager's actual comments after an annual appraisal discussion. He was obviously distraught. Let's examine the situation to try for a better result.

Crying is a learned response differing in men and women. For the most part, men are taught not to display their emotions. Young girls, on the other hand, are generally subjected to a different parental standard, and many learn that they often get their way if they cry. (This difference is starting to diminish. Young people in general now seem to have a healthier attitude about expressing emotions.) But for the time being, managers should be prepared for the possibility of tears from a female employee and take steps to minimize the discomfort.

In the situation just described, the male manager might consider these points. He should not inform the woman too far in advance about an upcoming appraisal discussion. Her concerned anticipation may raise her tension level to the point where tears may be the only relief. A day's notice is probably enough. Second, the discussion should not be a long one, belaboring in a pussyfooting fashion many points about needed improvement. Day-to-day interactions will take care of the details. At the annual appraisal, she should know first what the manager's overall judgments are about her work. Then he could go on to pinpoint a talent of hers to be developed or a new skill that's required. In this way, his suggestions are viewed in the light of his total evaluation, and she is not sitting there throughout the session wondering whether on the whole he is pleased or displeased. Finally, it's best not to be too gentle, too private, or too uninterrupted. A more direct approach may stir resentment rather than tears, which may be easier for both to handle. A phone call or two may take the heat off for a few moments, thus allowing her time to regain composure.

The manager should be prepared to handle the situation if she does cry. He might put a box of tissues on the table and say, "Mary, I know you don't want to cry, but this is a little hard on you. Just stay here a few minutes. I have to check on something. I'll be back in about five minutes." And then he should get up and leave the room. If when he returns her emotions are checked and he still has material to cover, he should do so. If she still shows some lack of control, he might say, "Let's get back together tomorrow." In the interim, she might be given something to do that requires physical exertion so that she can work off the feeling of strain.

Women can help themselves in this matter. Fear that she'll cry makes her boss dread giving her his reactions to her work, so it is to her advantage to find a way to forestall an outburst. Tears are due at least in part to tension. She might try to reduce it by being particularly active physically before an appraisal session. If she feels like crying during the meeting, she might say, "Joe, may I excuse myself? I'll be back in just a few minutes." If in spite of herself tears come anyway, she can say simply, "I'm sorry. This is difficult for you. Could we continue tomorrow?"

Women and Career Opportunities

When we ask a woman why she cried at an appraisal discussion, she usually says something like this: "I tried so hard on that project, but it didn't please him." This is part of the attitudinal change needed in going from nonprofessional to professional work, for which the standard is seldom based on effort but on results.

Perhaps one of the best ways to avoid tears at appraisal time is for a woman to appraise her own work results so that the manager is placed in a position where he can select one or two points for deeper exploration or counsel. This puts the woman in charge, giving her a sense of dignity; and if she covers a subject well, the manager avoids the judgmental function on that issue and places himself in the role of counselor or concerned associate.

Voices. The feminine voice can be most pleasant; or its pitch can at times be irritating and annoying—even to other women. A woman can help herself by not calling to someone across the office, by avoiding shrieks of laughter or giggles when with a group of women in areas where others are trying to work, and by using the intercom instead of shouting to her secretary from her office. On the other hand, she should be sure that she projects her voice sufficiently in meetings for others to hear her. These are small matters; but since problems can come up in this area, a little tact and thoughtfulness will minimize or eliminate them. Proper use of the voice is a skill, and if a woman's isn't effective, she might consider taking lessons from a professional. It may be a fortunate investment in her future.

Emotionalism. The industrial world understands male anger, but it is not very tolerant of hurt feelings. "She takes things personally" and "She isn't rational on this subject" are among the comments men make about women co-workers. Men are also hurt sometimes, of course; they take things per-

CAREER MANAGEMENT

sonally and become irrational. But pointing this out doesn't help the woman's situation. Here are two recommendations for women: emotionalism usually indicates sensitivity, so it should be capitalized on; and the emotions should be channeled into some productive activity that will benefit the company.

1. *Capitalize on sensitivity.* Helping men recognize the feelings expressed (often in an indirect fashion) by their male associates is an important part of manager training. They are taught that any message comes in two parts—the feeling and the information—and that if one deals with the feeling first, there's a better chance for joint constructive thinking about the information. If a woman is skilled at recognizing feelings in others, she has an advantage. Carl Rogers and the nondirective counselors could be studied, as well as Norman Maier's approach to the problem-solving interview.[1]

2. *Let the group help.* If a woman finds herself becoming emotional or irrational or projecting too much from personal feelings and she knows the people with whom she's dealing very well, she should stop talking, look at the group, and say, "I seem to be emotional on this subject. I wonder why? What affected me? I must think about this." This may bring about a confrontation within the group that will help everyone, including the woman. A male manager aware that a woman employee is becoming overly emotional shouldn't say, "Stop being emotional, Kay. We have to make a rational decision here!" That will merely put Kay on the defensive. He could say instead, "Let me see if I can state your feelings on this so that we'll be sure to take them into account here." Then he should do so. This probably gives him the best chance

---

[1] See Norman R. F. Maier, *Problem-Solving Discussions and Conferences* (New York: McGraw-Hill, 1963); Carl R. Rogers, *Counseling and Psychotherapy* (Boston: Houghton Mifflin, 1942).

to deal with the situation effectively and move Kay on to a more constructive approach.

Sexual responsiveness. Men sometimes feel that women flaunt their sexuality on the job in a way that distracts them from work and that they find personally disturbing. Certainly, the last thing most men want is to deny a woman's femininity. In fact, they're very critical of the woman who tries to imitate men, who becomes overly aggressive and domineering in her efforts to advance her career. A woman can accept her femininity and still help herself by dressing appropriately for the work she does. She should also avoid trying to win favors and advantages by applying old-fashioned feminine wiles.

There will still be times when a man will respond sexually to a woman with whom he is working or when a woman will so react to a male associate. Such responsiveness can actually help the working relationship and improve communication between the two, provided they handle the matter with maturity. But fair is fair. It's a good rule to keep one's private life out of the office and to make personal standards as clear at work as after hours. Attempts to lure a married person away from his or her spouse are violations of professionalism in working relationships. A woman's career is not helped much and is sometimes limited by her inability to keep relationships on a friendly and compatible but still clearly work-oriented basis.

Physiological problems. A particular complaint of managers about female employees is of monthly absences because of the menstrual period. The fact that not all women take time off for this reason is ignored in the men's irritation over those who do. Responsible medical advice indicates that for most women the onset of menstruation is a time of some discomfort but one to which most become accustomed by the time they're old enough to accept a job. If a female employee is consistently absent for this reason, her manager might suggest that she get medical advice. Working women should seek and follow the advice of a competent physician. Many women find, however, that being fully occupied is likely to be the best antidote for pain or discomfort.

The menstrual period may also be accompanied by a somewhat higher tension level, which may result in stronger emotional reactions. A woman who finds this true of herself should probably avoid delicate discussions or very difficult decisions during this time that require her to be at her best, assuming that such matters can be delayed without penalty. When they cannot, she will need to take extra care and time to handle them well. Mere awareness of possible problems may help one circumvent unusually irritable responses, loss of composure, and so on. These simple precautions apply to both *men* and women when something throws them off balance, causing them to feel more than usual stress.

The second physiological problem that can affect women is the menopause period. Modern medicine provides so many aids for avoiding serious discomfort and states of anxiety and depression that the best advice is to seek competent gynecological assistance. The evidence seems to be, however, that the menopause period is a good time for a woman to be working. She is in contact with other people, involved in responsible work, and less likely to be self-absorbed than the woman who remains at home with a great deal of time to think about herself.

Since this is usually a difficult time for a woman psychologically, her manager should try to express support and confidence more than usual. Her ego needs bolstering. If the woman is working for an understanding man, it may be best for her to sit down with him when both are relaxed and talk to him about her problem. This is something about which neither needs to feel embarrassed. It is an area where communication can be improved so that mutually helpful decisions and actions can be taken.

The working mother. The working mother simply has certain commitments that take precedence over her work—the care and raising of her children. Anyone who hires a working mother must be prepared to accept her priorities and be sure the work requirements are compatible with it. Working mothers must be certain the employer understands these priorities and that the work will not suffer because of them.

The Woman Manager

Inevitably, the day will come in a firm when some woman with managerial interests and abilities will be appointed to a supervisory post and men will be working for her. Here are a few suggestions for this woman to help her over this difficult hurdle.

Entertain the man and his wife. It's often difficult for a man to explain to his wife that he works for a woman. So as soon as possible, his boss should entertain the members of her staff with their wives or husbands so that they get to know her personally. Once they become aware of her competence, they will understand why she warrants a responsible position. She should also let the wives know—in specific terms—how capable their husbands are.

Demonstrate interest in the man's longer-term career. As soon after her appointment as possible, a woman manager ought to sit down with each person who reports to her to explore his career interests and assure him of her personal wish to help him display his best capabilities. This helps the man realize that his tenure under her is not a "life sentence" and that she intends to promote his interests actively.

CAREER MANAGEMENT

Give employees visibility among higher-level management. Whenever one of her employees does an especially good piece of work, she would do well to create an opportunity for him to explain it to *her* boss. She should urge her superior and her associates to deal directly with employees on matters in which they have expertise. She needn't insist on all things being channeled through her. She could send samples of good work or complimentary letters to upper management and make sure the employee involved knows she's done it.

Move employees on to better jobs. She should single out employees with potential to do better work and, when they're ready for upward advancement, help them to better positions. This establishes her reputation as a source of excellent promotable people even though it places an extra training burden on her.

Keep your femininity. A woman can let employees know she is tough-minded enough to help them grow and enhance the reputation of the organization without being tough for its own sake. Like any other good manager, she should display warmth and appreciation of human values. She should be considerate of employees' time. She can make them feel welcome in her office, and she can go to their work areas when that is more appropriate. She can find a pleasant word or two to say in a chance meeting and can remember to inquire about families and personal interests.

Play no favorites. She must be absolutely fair in her treatment of subordinates. She needn't lean over backward to accommodate men at the expense of women but should treat both with respect and warmth.

In short, a woman can be a manager on her own terms, using her personal strengths and acting out of her own clearly communicated philosophy.

9

Senior Employees

It is commonplace for manuals dealing with older employees to suggest that a career is probably about over by the late 50s or early 60s. Most of us undoubtedly know people who decide to wait out the last five to ten years before retirement. These can become the longest, dullest, most difficult years in a person's life, with little to keep him going but anticipation of the "glorious" retirement ahead. (That the retirement is seldom exactly glorious is well known.) Often the aging process becomes more noticeable during this period as the energy level decreases with lack of interest.

This chapter will not explore geriatrics or argue the merits of outstanding contributions by older people. Rather, it will assume that most individuals are capable of high-level performance up to and past retirement, that the last five years in anyone's career can be highly productive, and that continued self-actualization is therefore desired and desirable. Consequently, we shall discuss how we can make the working environment of the last career stages stimulating and rewarding. Specifically, we'll consider ways to package work for the older employee, the importance of day-to-day interaction with him, special performance appraisals and career discussions, prestige and recognition for the senior performer, and initiatives a younger manager can take to improve relationships. We'll also review some of the things the older man can avoid in order to help himself: discouraging new ideas, living in the past, rambling when making a point, and holding the reins too long. Finally, we'll recommend things he can do in order to carry his career through to a suitable close or to the point of transition to a new working experience.

Facilitating the Older Employee's Career

Packaging Work with Age in Mind

A manager usually has considerable freedom to design his department and structure the positions of those reporting to him. Here are a few ground rules to help him improve the productivity and maintain the career progress of older employees.

Make a closer match between man and job. A manager ought to assign a bright young employee to work that represents an attainable level of difficulty but that nonetheless requires considerable stretch. This encourages him to add to his knowledge and skills quite rapidly. In dealing with the older employee, however, the manager needs to make a closer match. To the extent possible, he should capitalize on the man's demonstrated past performance, thus putting him to work on commitments he is currently capable of meeting with excellence. This accomplishes several objectives: the work produced is likely to be outstanding, which is good for the organization; the employee will appear capable and successful to his associates and to himself, which benefits his self-confidence and motivation; the man is reassured about his capability at a time of life that can be threatening to him; and the level of his personal involvement in the goals and products of the organization is probably sustained because of his contribution.

Exhibit 2 shows a systematic method for checking the match between job and man.

Require quality improvement. Aligning a job with a man's capabilities does not mean one should assign tasks that require him to repeat work he's done many times before. A wise manager will build on the senior employee's past experience, but will also ask for a greater contribution in terms of quality—a better job or a different application—rather than faster results. Time pressure is often harder on a senior man than on a younger one. But asking for an improvement in the caliber of the work he has done in the past is likely to arouse his interest. A manager needs imagination to devise work with moderate opportunity for growth. He might try putting a problem directly into the hands of a capable older man. "Pete," he might say, "you're the only person in this department who might be interested enough and willing to take the time to find a way to remove the red tape from our ordering system without sacrificing our good control over price. Would you take a look at it to see if you can find an easier way, one that cuts down on paperwork?" Our suggestion that the manager pose such a problem does not imply that the assignment would be of low priority. A capable senior employee would immediately perceive this as make-work, and the task would discourage him even if it were economically feasible. Instead, a high-priority assignment is needed, one that wouldn't be done at all if a fully experienced individual were not available to do it.

Exhibit 2. Checklist for matching man and job.

Job Requirements	Man Possesses (Check the appropriate column.)		
	To a High Degree	To a Moderate Degree	Very Little
1. Knowledge of			
_____	_____	_____	_____
_____	_____	_____	_____
_____	_____	_____	_____
2. Skills in			
_____	_____	_____	_____
_____	_____	_____	_____
_____	_____	_____	_____
3. Relationships with (list other related jobs)			
_____	_____	_____	_____
_____	_____	_____	_____
_____	_____	_____	_____
4. Demonstrated ability to (list key work goals)			
_____	_____	_____	_____
_____	_____	_____	_____
_____	_____	_____	_____
5. Other			
_____	_____	_____	_____
_____	_____	_____	_____
_____	_____	_____	_____

Examine the check marks above. For the older employee, most of the check marks should fall in the first two columns if the job requirement is a serious one and if rapid or complex learning is involved.

Set short work cycles. The next step is to make assignments short enough so that the employee experiences success rather frequently. A manager should deliberately assign projects that can be completed within, say, two or three months. If the nature of the work doesn't permit this, he should divide it into several segments of about that duration each and follow through with the man, segment by segment. Such short assignments or segments help the man sustain his interest, and his feelings of satisfaction and importance increase at each successful accomplishment.

Ask for frequent reports. If such a segmented assignment were to be given to a man in midcareer, a manager might well ask nothing about it until some major phase were completed or scheduled for completion. For an employee in his preretirement years, the need for companionship, reassurances, and a sense of playing an important position on the team may be critical. Requesting the man to give an informal, five-minute, oral report describing what he is doing and how it is coming can fill this need. The report might be given to his associates at a regular staff meeting or some similar, likely occasion.

Informal Personal Contacts

Often a manager avoids his older employees. He finds some of their remarks and work habits difficult to deal with, to say nothing of their attitudes. This can isolate the older man, confirming his feelings of unimportance. Frequent contacts, on the other hand, can reassure the man that he is liked, respected, and considered a much-needed part of the team. So the manager who is really interested in sustaining career development will devise a system that reminds him to see older employees. Contacts need not and probably should not be long ones. The key is to express interest and relay information informally, thus giving a man some advance notice of changes that may lie ahead. For the older person does not like to be caught short; he may not be so flexible as he once was and may need a longer recovery or adjustment time. Catching him off guard may so disturb him that his performance suffers and his behavior changes noticeably for the worse.

If the employee is one in whom the manager can safely confide, so much the better. This kind of relationship is indicative of mutual liking and respect and usually engenders in the employee a desire to do his best. Since most managers need someone to serve as a sounding board, the relationship is close to ideal. It may allow the manager to resolve his problems. At the same time, it provides the employee with advance information that he can use to good advantage. This, in turn, increases the odds of his success and helps to place him in the manager's inner circle of confidants.

Performance Appraisals for the Senior Man

It has become something of a tradition in American industry to space performance appraisal discussions with the senior employee farther and farther apart. Presumably, most recommendations would be repetitions of old ones, and he would either have taken successful action by now or long since have given up efforts to improve in a particular area. However, in view of his needs for reassurance and support during his late 50s and early 60s, this may well be the wrong period for less frequent man-manager assessments accompanied by a projection of implications for his future.

For this reason, it is recommended that appraisal discussions be held at six-month intervals. The use of management by objectives permits a backward look at the end of six months

Senior Employees

to evaluate specific results he was asked to achieve during the period. Since these will have changed each time, the material will be fresh. Here are a few suggestions for handling the discussion.

Ask for a briefing from the employee. Begin by asking the man to brief you on his feelings about his work during the last six months. What is he proud of? What does he believe might have brought more success? In the case of a senior professional, such an evaluation may well be more penetrating than your own analysis. When he makes an assessment with which you agree—either favorable or unfavorable—make sure you let him know this and select a specific action or accomplishment of his to illustrate your confirmation. If you find yourself in disagreement, don't contradict him. Say simply, "I've looked at this matter a little differently. Let's see why we disagree on this." Ask him why he feels as he does; then you explain why you feel as you do. Try, then, to reconcile your views so that this kind of disagreement doesn't occur in the future.

Point out future implications. Be both objective and supportive in helping the man understand the implications of his performance for future work assignments, salary reviews, development plans, and career progress. Yes, cover *all* these things just as you would for a much younger man.

Obtain work assignment suggestions. To the extent possible, try to draw from the man whatever suggestions he may have for ways to use his talents that would meet company commitments and contribute substantially to decision making for the overall organization. In doing this, the proper attitude is not to appear that you're out for his last drop of blood before he retires but rather to show that his remaining time is precious to you both and you want and need very much the benefit of his mature contributions. You want to be sure, therefore, that you have overlooked no facet of his experience or interest in planning the work he will be doing.

Discuss salary recommendations. Even if it is not customary to discuss salary at appraisal time, it is a good idea to let the senior employee know that he is still being reviewed and what the administrative procedures are in his case. If he is at the top of the salary range for his position, for example, you should point this out and say, "Larry, you know your salary is top of the scale for your job, so no increase will be possible when you're next reviewed. But it must be a great satisfaction to you to know that your contribution is considered to be tops as well. In your case, your performance and pay match perfectly." Don't lie, of course; but if it is true, say it.

Include development plans. In preparing for the discussion, pick something quite specific for the man to work on, some knowledge to be refreshed or updated or added or some skill to be further refined. There is in fact no greater reassurance than to let the man know you haven't given up on him, that you still expect change and improvement. He may grumble a bit or seem irritated. That's unimportant. What will come through to him for the most part is that you are still treating him like the developing man he really is, and this will basically be a positive, reinforcing experience for him.

Suggest career plans. An older man facing a substantial career change in the not too distant future will probably be more thoughtful, more exploratory, and more specific about what it is he wishes to accomplish both before and after the change. The former is within your province, so your discussion can be pretty direct, containing as many ideas and suggestions as you can produce from your own thinking or awaken in him. The period after the change is of course the man's personal management concern, so your probing should go forward only to the extent that he is willing to talk about it. Since the career discussion is often neglected with the older employee, let's take a special look at it.

Career Discussions with Older Employees

The purpose of discussing a young man's career with him is twofold: to obtain facts for the promotion system so that his abilities and interests are considered as openings occur, and to provide information that will help him make realistic decisions and choices for himself. Presumably, management assumes that the young man has a working lifetime with the firm ahead of him worth serious discussion, exploration, and planning. In fact, however, a high percentage of young employees leave their current employers after two or three years. Thus the 58-year-old man who has seven years to work before retirement may be a surer bet for continued employment than the younger man, and discussing his career may actually have greater payoff in that plans made for him can in fact be implemented and their effects seen in the firm.

So the career discussion is worth special consideration, even at this late stage of the man's development. For the senior employee, most speculation about him is over. Both he and his manager have a pretty clear idea of how his talents have matured in both rate and direction. Openings that are likely to occur are nearer at hand, and it is easier to estimate their requirements.

The basic question, then, "What do you envision as the best possible job for you two years from now?" has double importance. His answer gives you an idea of what expectation level the man still has for himself, and this, if it is reasonable, may suggest new positions for which he might qualify or changes in the current job that might offer more satisfaction from daily work.

That level of expectation might be for a lower-paid job, a less complex one, or one physically less demanding. If his reasons for the desired change are sound, they should certainly be honored and perhaps encouraged. The American image of a career that starts at the bottom, rises to some glorious peak, and then plateaus out is ridiculous in an age in which knowledge increases at such a rapid rate. A career curve that starts low, reaches some optimum for the individual, and then gently trails lower may in fact be much more livable. But this requires value changes so that careers can decline in responsibility, physical demand, and presumably monetary reward without loss of honor or the need to find face-saving devices. Since this vision of career progress has not yet been realized, to whatever extent the employee himself wants changes leading toward a less demanding situation, the manager will be wise to cooperate if possible.

Prestige and Recognition

Other cultures have done much better than ours in honoring their elders. There is a great need to find ways to give the senior employee some well-earned prestige and recognition for not only past but current accomplishments. At a time when salary increases may be difficult to support administratively, other forms of recognition become especially important.

There are often worthwhile community assignments that carry prestige and may be best suited to the mature, knowledgeable employee. Not only could he represent his firm well but he may meet others in similar situations who might be helpful in forming his retirement plans.

Senior Employees

Asking the senior employee to chair certain internal meetings gives him a place of honor while others carry out the tougher, more demanding tasks on the program.

You might also name him deputy in your absence with responsibility to review mail and handle telephone requests. Ask him to substitute for you at certain meetings and report back the proceedings. Invite him to attend meetings in which his experience is useful even though his position in the organization might not qualify him. Awards of merit for special projects can be useful whether or not they carry a monetary honorarium. A small luncheon on his company anniversary date is in good taste and usually welcomed, as is an occasional casual invitation to lunch with you personally or as part of a small group. All these things tell him more plainly than words that he is still a valued member of the team. You might kid him or tease him if he starts reminiscing about the good old days or viewing the future with great alarm. Humor often works when impatience or sarcasm would destroy him.

There are some avenues to avoid as well. Don't load him with worthless assignments in order to give him a feeling of prestige. More than likely, he'll recognize their lack of value, and his confidence will be undermined rather than bolstered. Keep the percentage of special assignments within reason—20 to 30 percent of the total at the outside. If too many are given, the man is likely to feel (and be) outside the mainstream of the department's work. Finally, it is probably unwise to give a much older man the task of helping new, young college graduates make the transition to working life. The gap is too great. The pace of the older man is slower; he is likely to throw cold water on new ideas and dampen enthusiasm. Although there are always exceptions to the rule, limiting his circle of major influence to a group within 10 to 15 years of his own age is usually a sound idea.

CAREER MANAGEMENT

The Young Manager and the Older Man

All the foregoing suggestions in this chapter have been equally applicable to the young and the middle-aged manager to whom a senior employee reports. When the age gap is quite wide, however, the young manager often experiences special difficulties with the older man. They usually grow out of one of two extreme attitudes of his own. The first is the demonstrated or expressed notion that everyone past 50 is over the hill and ought to get out of the way for the good of the organization. The second is a feeling of hesitancy about how much he ought to ask of the older man, how much guidance he personally can give him, and whether the employee will accept him as his manager.

Get the facts on aging. If you find you hold such attitudes, logic alone won't change them. But you can help yourself by getting facts. Talk to a company physician, if one is available, to learn about the general effects of aging. In a specific case, ask the older employee to have a physical examination so that both of you have the recommendations of a doctor to guide you.

Next, make sure you and the man agree on the specific work he is to do, when he will do it, and how it will be measured. This will enable you to judge his performance on facts rather than on personal impressions gained during meetings.

If you find the association so unbearable that you're likely to be unable to conceal your feelings when the two of you are together, find someone in the office more tolerant to whom you can entrust the personal contact function of your job in this one case. Just acknowledge that this is time-consuming, and make it a recognized part of his job for which there will be some reward if the work is done well.

This delegation of responsibility may seem a mistake to

many. Indeed, in most cases, a young manager should be able to respect his associates and show it. But occasionally, for many deep-seated reasons, a young man just cannot contain his impatience. He may simply take away all the joy of working from his older colleague, who may not at this point be able to make a job move as a younger man could. When this happens or is likely to happen, a go-between should be considered, mainly on humane grounds but with the good of the organization in mind as well.

Deal with personal insecurity. If you display insecurity in handling an older associate, you probably accentuate any feelings he may have had that you were not ready for the job. So again, get sound medical advice, both general and specific, and base your demands on it. Next, assume consent in the relationship. Take it for granted that the man recognizes you were selected and he was excluded for sound reasons. Assume he wants and needs your facilitating work to help him get his job done.

If you are reasonably sure he feels he should have had your job, invite him to express this to you openly. Say to him, for example, "John, I'm concerned about your career. Did you feel that you should have had this job?" Then be quiet and let him express his feelings. You may be surprised and relieved to learn that he had no such thought at all. Or he may feel that it's a young man's world and that unfair decisions are made on the basis of age alone. It is probably best for him to get this view fully articulated. When he appears to be finished, you might want to say something like this: "John, I'm sorry you feel this way, but I'm glad you've shared it with me. Now the important thing to do is work together to set up your job so that it displays your talents to their best advantage. I'll need your help to do this, so let's both think it over and sit down together soon to work out a plan that's solid. How about it? How soon can we get together?" This sort of discussion should place you in a consultative, supportive role that should eliminate much of the uncertainty you felt earlier. It also gives John a status he can live with.

Ways the Mature Employee Can Help Himself

A man reaching his late 50s or early 60s can avoid a number of behavior patterns that irritate associates on the job. Most such restraints call for self-discipline. They require caring about the relationships one builds on the job and caring enough to take these actions. They take self-attention and self-awareness so that the occasion requiring restraint is recognized as well as the course of action to be taken. A well-adjusted older person, aware of his probable failings, may even set up a few insurance policies in advance. He may say, "I'm given to wandering from the point, so if I do it in talking with you, just remind me we're talking about another subject." But most are hesitant to expose themselves this way, and most people so requested are unwilling to hurt the feelings of their older associate.

Here are a few suggestions for overcoming certain habits that others find annoying.

Remain open to ideas, new or old. Young people often attempt things tried many times before because they aren't aware of failures. So they approach a problem from a new viewpoint and with enthusiasm, and they sometimes succeed in finding a new, workable solution. One of the distressing signals of a man's advancing age is his patiently pointing out that something cannot be done for very good reasons and then giving a detailed history of previous trials and failures. The suggestion here is to resist the inclination to do this and instead say, "Try it, try it—only way to find out!" This assumes, of course, that the cost of trying is not enormous and that the risks run will not jeopardize the organization.

Concentrate on the future. "Back in 1930 we had a great time . . ." becomes wearisome indeed to the hearer. Unless someone asks what happened at some point in the past, save your memories for friends of the same age, family, or the editor of your memoirs. Consciously try to allot a good part of your working conversation to contemplating the next year, the next decade, or the next century. And if you possibly can, do so with anticipation and enthusiasm. Plan your work to include its probable application one to five years from now. Ask for some assignments involving long-range planning, and give your imagination a workout thinking ahead and predicting future events.

Come to the point. The long-winded, circuitous way to the point bores listeners. Pretty soon they are thinking their own thoughts while you ramble on. If you're going to comment on something, make advance notes of what you want to say and force yourself to stick to them. For off-the-cuff commentary, look at your watch and limit your remarks to one or two minutes at a time. If you're not making the point clear so that you feel you're losing an important argument, say simply, "I'm not expressing myself well. Would you delay the decision overnight and let me put my thoughts on paper?"

Initiate change in your responsibilities. If you have indications from your boss or associates that they feel you're trying to continue to do a job that has become too much for you, initiate a discussion about a change in your responsibilities. If your boss feels it's too soon for a change, he'll tell you. But be prepared with suggestions of work that will continue to be satisfying to you even if it is less demanding. You might consider, for example, consultant responsibilities instead of managerial ones or a smaller group if you've had a big one. Or take on a project that you've been interested in for some time but that never seems to get done, and let someone else carry your job while you do it.

"Leave the job while you're still ahead" should be your motto. The manager who holds the reins too long is just as sorry a sight as the athlete who plays past his prime. Since you may not know when this moment has arrived for you, you need a good friend or a good boss or an outside counselor to tell you. Make arrangements for this kind of help before the time comes when you need the advice. Then you can both talk about it more freely and discuss how you'll handle any (quite natural) bad feelings you might express when the moment actually arrives and you are advised to change.

Make notes. Start the habit of taking notes and preparing agendas early so you won't feel awkward when they become a necessity.

Cooperate with your physician. Work with a physician who is interested in the aging process and will follow your personal physiological and emotional changes with constructive concern. He will suggest changes in work patterns, extracurricular efforts, diet, and similar matters. These can prolong the number of active years and make the transition to a less active life easier.

Pass along your experience. It could prove valuable to capture the experience you've gained throughout your working life, package it, and leave it for the use of others. If you are the sort to write a book, you might try your hand at it. If you prefer to talk, buy a tape recorder and, talking from an outline, tell what you know. Or find an interested junior in the firm and pass along some of your experiences to him by word of mouth. Or perhaps you can get someone to put them into a series of reports, instructions, or procedures. At least, go through your files with a competent clerk and destroy the accumulation of useless materials, consolidating the best under a set of descriptive headings. The kind of work you've done dictates what to document. If, for example, you're a technical specialist, your reports and designs probably speak for themselves. If you're an executive, you've probably transmitted your knowledge through personal example over the years. But do take time to determine what your most valuable experiences have been and how they can best be passed along to your successors.

Make retirement plans. Sometimes the best way to transmit experience is by making it available to other kinds of organizations, various institutions, or perhaps other countries where expertise of your special variety is less developed. It's unlikely that, if you have had a good career, one that has been personally satisfying and rewarding, you can drop it once you reach a certain age and do nothing constructive with your life from that point on. So it's a good idea to have a plan in mind for what you will do when the time comes to retire. Lay the groundwork while you're still on the job by making the necessary contacts for your next career or the next phase of your career. This, too, will keep you oriented toward the future, and while you may not—in fact, should not—discuss it at great length while at work, the fact that you are planning and taking steps for your future will reinforce your sense of personal worth and enhance your image among your associates as a contributing member of today's and tomorrow's society.

10

A Manager Training Program

"John, I have an offer from another company. I'd like to discuss it with you and talk about my opportunities here so that I can make the right decision."

A manager hearing these words often freezes. He dreads this discussion. He foresees a long, difficult search to replace the present employee and an irritating, time-consuming break-in period once someone is hired. He hastily tries to think of something to say to the man about opportunities. He may feel a little guilty that he hasn't proposed and supported him vigorously for a better job within the firm. His first reaction may be to consider what he can do about giving him a salary increase ("Let's see. How long *has* it been?") or upgrading the job on the salary scale by a notch or two.

Instead of dealing with this situation solely as an information- and action-provoking process, he might well consider

A Manager Training Program

its emotional aspects also. What is this employee feeling at the moment? What brought about the offer? Did the employee seek it out because of personal dissatisfaction with his present position? Is he using it as leverage to force the manager to talk about future prospects? These are important factors that will help guide the course of any discussion between the two men. We'll take a look at one way this dialog might be handled in the next chapter. The intention here is to stress two points: (1) The manager caught off guard responds as best he can. But he would be in a much stronger position if the discussion were carried out in a less threatening climate. The employee, too, would be better off if he had thought through his general situation before he faced the pressure of a specific offer. (2) Managers need both information and training in order to conduct helpful career discussions with employees.

These points suggest that the career-facilitating system of a firm should include periodic discussions with employees to learn of their current interests, to provide information about likely opportunities, job requirements, and the like, and to work out alternate paths to known career targets. Such discussions are best carried out by trained counselors—professionals in a personnel or manager development function. However, most firms cannot provide this service because of cost and inadequate numbers of competent specialists. Moreover, many employees are unwilling to seek and pay for outside help of this nature. Perhaps they should be encouraged to do so.

The manager therefore finds himself charged with the responsibility more often than not. The least he deserves is training to establish the probable limits of the help he can give, to provide some approaches for dealing with situations that arise frequently, and to help him find suitable words to ask for needed information and respond to it. In this chapter, a suggested training program is outlined. It contains a considerable amount of practice in actual discussion since only through practice can the manager begin to feel some degree of confidence in his ability to deal with this extraordinarily delicate type of interview.

The training program is presented in outline form. It is planned for 20 to 25 participants. It consists of six sessions. Sessions 1, 2, 3, 4, and 6 are planned for approximately two hours each. Session 5 takes three hours. Depending on the interest of participants and their beginning level of sophistication, sessions 4 and 5 may each be expanded into two sessions to give more opportunity for practice with group review and critique. It is assumed that the instructor is experienced in lecturing, leading group and case discussions, and counseling. Video taping is suggested. If it's not available, audio recording can be done, but much of the nonverbal communication will of course be lost. Since participants usually wish to view their own tapes, provision for additional showing between sessions should be made. Over time, a small library of good tapes could be built up to serve as examples of how to discuss careers. Participants' permission must be gotten to show tapes in which they appear or are heard personally.

SESSION 1. Objective: To help the manager understand his role in career management and establish his values with respect to advancing employees' careers.

Introductory comments. "We are beginning today to explore a managerial work area about which there is considerable disagreement and the nature of which is in fact undergoing very rapid change. Today we want to discuss and try to understand the problem of career advancement—the firm's role, the employee's role, and your personal role. Specifically, with respect to your role, we are going to investigate your beliefs about people that influence your attitude toward your associates and that give life and meaning to everything you do and say about helping them reach their working goals. In the second and third sessions, we'll make sure you know the exact workings of our promotion system, the information available to each of you about the people who report to you, whatever data we have on job families and career patterns, the information available about the direction our business is taking, and the likely opportunities that will present themselves during the next 5 to 10 years. Finally, we're going to ask you to consider the adequacy of this information to determine whether you need more in order to fulfill your responsibilities and, if so, from whom it might be obtained or how developed.

"In the fourth session, we'll get down to work on typical though dramatized cases requiring career discussion. We'll suggest a general format or approach and ask you to role-play, in this way helping each other improve your skills in relating to people so as to generate more meaningful dialog. We'll video-tape some of these role-playing sessions so that you can see yourselves in action.

"Finally, in the fifth session, we'll ask some of our new young employees to help us by playing themselves, interested in discussing their careers. We'd like each of you to hold a real-life discussion with a member of your organization during the month following session 5, tape it, and then return for a wrap-up session to exchange experiences. As you see, we've programmed a six-session course extending over a period of about two and a half months.

"Would you begin by reading the list of questions I'm handing out [see Exhibit 3]? Circle the choice of response to each question that most nearly matches your feeling on the subject. Then we'll outline the next step."

Exercise (1¼ hours). Participants answer the question-

Exhibit 3. Career values questionnaire.

For statements 1–13, circle the answer that most closely represents your opinion.

1. *I believe the company has an obligation to provide a lifetime career for every employee who joins it.*
   I agree.   There are important exceptions.   I disagree.

2. *I believe that every person should have made his career choice by the time he is 30 years old.*
   I agree.   There are important exceptions.   I disagree.

3. *By the age of 50, a person should stop thinking about a better job.*
   I agree.   There are important exceptions.   I disagree.

4. *Young college graduates today want to get ahead too fast. They need to learn patience on their first job.*
   I agree.   There are important exceptions.   I disagree.

5. *Women belong in the home. If they must work, they should learn some specialty and stay out of managing.*
   I agree.   There are important exceptions.   I disagree.

6. *I have to be able to tell the people who report to me what better jobs they can do after this one.*
   I agree.   There are important exceptions.   I disagree.

7. *If an employee sets his career goals too high, I owe it to him to tell him so.*
   I agree.   There are important exceptions.   I disagree.

8. *Employees don't have to tell me their career aspirations. It's none of my business.*
   I agree.   There are important exceptions.   I disagree.

9. *We need administrative ground rules about how fast an employee can move from one job to the other.*
   I agree.   There are important exceptions.   I disagree.

A Manager Training Program

Exhibit 3, cont'd.

---

10. *If an employee is essential to the success of an important piece of work, I cannot in good conscience recommend him for or let him take on a promotional opportunity.*
    I agree.   There are important exceptions.   I disagree.

11. *I'm responsible for the career choices of employees who report to me.*
    I agree.   There are important exceptions.   I disagree.

12. *Personnel people run the promotion system. I don't have any responsibility for it.*
    I agree.   There are important exceptions.   I disagree.

13. *I can tell as soon as I meet a man how far up the organization ladder he's likely to go.*
    I agree.   There are important exceptions.   I disagree.

Write your answers to questions 14 and 15.

14. At what age did you decide on the career in which you now find yourself? (For example, if you are a manager, when did you decide you wanted to manage the sort of work you're engaged in; if an engineer, when did you decide on the kind of engineering you're doing; if a computer service manager, when did you decide computer servicing was for you?) How long ago was this?

---

15. Think about former managers. Without giving his name, can you identify the one who most helped advance your career? What did he do that helped?

147

naire. Then divide them into small groups of five or six. Ask them to engage in a leaderless discussion on the first 13 questions to see whether they can reach agreement. If they cannot agree except by rewriting a statement, they should rewrite it. If they feel there are important exceptions, they should record the two or three most important ones. Since time will not permit all groups to discuss all questions, assign them as follows:

Group 1: Questions 1–4
Group 2: Questions 4–7
Group 3: Questions 7–10
Group 4: Questions 10–13

The overlap will allow groups to check how closely the thinking of one agrees with another. They can also leave the overlap question until last so that if time runs out, all questions will probably be covered.

Group discussion (45 minutes). Begin by having each person state the age at which he decided on his present career and how long ago. Get an average and a range on age and an average on time elapsed since the decision. It is quite probable that the age will vary with the participant's age and that it is relatively recently that the profession reflected in his current job was chosen. The point for the group is that careers usually (not always) involve a fairly continuous series of decisions; it is a fallacy to think that a stance is taken early in life and then some great master plan is drawn up and followed. Rather, at each step most of us consolidate our gains for a while and then begin to contemplate the next move.

Then lead a discussion on answers to question 15. Make a blackboard list of actions or attitudes that had a favorable influence. From this you can probably draw a pretty clear

A Manager Training Program

picture of the desirable role for managers in facilitating career advancement. Star items of the manager's role that will be covered in succeeding sessions.

Collect the value statements that each group prepared, and tell participants they'll receive a consolidated list back within a couple of days for their own use.

Homework assignment. Each participant should rework the complete list of career value statements to reflect his personal beliefs on the subject. Each should retain his final copy for use throughout the course and for comparison with the consolidated group statement.

SESSION 2. Objective: To supply participants with useful information on the promotion system, the availability of data on employees, and past career patterns; to enlist their help in avoiding common abuses of the promotion system.

Introductory comments. "Your assignment this week was to review the career value statements and to rework them to express your own beliefs. If the values stated are honest, they should move you to take certain actions with respect to employee career advancement. One homework assignment you will be asked to complete after this and the next two sessions is a list of at least one specific action you will take to show your good intention regarding the 13 points. Before session 3, please do this for the first four statements. Any questions?

"Today's session essentially concerns receiving and digesting information. You need to be in possession of all the facts about our promotion system, how it is working, ways it is failing, and how you personally can help it function better. A good part of your discussion with employees about their careers will lay the groundwork of encouraging them to be candid in describing their personal goals so that you can remove obstacles from their paths and facilitate their personal career programming. To do this well, there is basic information you need to be thoroughly familiar with."

Lecture: The promotion system and job families (1 hour). The instructor should either present the facts himself or bring in someone from the personnel organization familiar with the practical day-to-day functioning of the promotion system. It is recommended that a short manual be handed out that includes all basic policies and instructions on the subject, the forms in use, and one or two actual (perhaps disguised) case histories. Any information on past career paths and natural job families that shows how one job prepares for one or more others should be included, along with a description of what is contained in official personnel files and what additional personnel data managers should consider keeping. Allow adequate time for questions and discussion.

Exercise (30 minutes). Present four of the most common abuses of the promotion system, using actual ones if possible. Then ask the participants to form small groups, assign one abuse to each, and let the participants discuss how it might be corrected. Perhaps include such common faults as these:

1. The manager conceals an outstanding performer in order to keep him.
2. The manager refuses to let an employee go to a better job because his work is essential at that particular time.
3. The employee and manager complete all paperwork connected with promotion recommendations, and then nothing happens.
4. The manager claims to consider candidates from outside his own department but always picks someone from inside.

Group reports (30 minutes). A spokesman for each of the groups reports the recommendations of his associates. The instructor promises to forward these recommendations to the appropriate policy maker whenever his action is required.

Homework assignment. Each participant should review the information discussed during this session. To reinforce it, he should include its content as an agenda item for a staff meeting to be held during the week with employees who report to him.

Reviewing career value statements 1–4, each participant should list at least one specific action he will take to implement his beliefs and give a date when he will do or begin it.

SESSION 3. Objective: To supply participants with useful information about the future of the business and likely job opportunities that should occur if plans materialize; to identify additional areas where information is needed in order to conduct career interest discussions intelligently.

Introductory comments. "Today's session will be devoted to two subject areas. The first is a description of our business plans to be sure that you are familiar with our current thoughts about the work that lies ahead and the manpower needs associated with it. The second is to examine our promotion system so that it is used intelligently and fairly."

Lecture: Business plans and future opportunities (45 minutes). The instructor, a business planner, a marketing manager, or someone familiar with the business plans of the firm should describe briefly the general direction the firm plans to take in the next 5 to 10 years. He must make it clear that this course is subject to change and involves considerable speculation and prediction. Then he and a personnel specialist (if one is available) together with the instructor should draw from these plans implications for the kinds of jobs likely to be needed. Once more, participants must be warned that there is considerable uncertainty about these projections. It is prob-

CAREER MANAGEMENT

ably best for them to make notes on this portion rather than to have literature supplied. Encourage questions, discussion, suggestions, and conclusions.

Exercise (45 minutes). Divide the participants into small groups to explore the following questions and make recommendations.

1. Are the promotion policy and system adequate from your point of view? Are there important changes you would like to see made in them to strengthen them from the point of view of the company, the employee, and the manager? List the most important of such changes.
2. What things can you do to make the system function better? List three specific actions you will take, projecting actual dates.
3. Do you have adequate information about projected business plans and how the promotion system functions to conduct career discussions? If not, list additional information you feel is essential.

Group reports (30 minutes). A spokesman for each group should present recommendations arising from the three questions. If possible, invite the personnel manager responsible for policy in this area to attend. Forward the recommendations to him for consideration and reply by the next meeting.

Homework assignment. Participants should review the information on business plans with its career implications and discuss it at their next staff meeting. This will reinforce the information for them as well as serve a communication purpose.

Reviewing career value statements 5–8, each participant should list at least one specific action he will take to implement his beliefs and give a date when he will do or begin it.

Each participant should review the official personnel file

A Manager Training Program

and any special information he has on two employees who report to him. If he needs to start files for his personal use, he should do so.

SESSION 4. Objective: To teach a viable pattern for real-life dialog through simulated career discussions; to help the participants develop some personal standards for questioning, listening, and counseling.

Preliminary. If there has been a written or oral reply to the recommendations made at the last session, make it known.

Introductory comments. "Today we begin work on personal relationships. It is not an easy task to institute new behavior patterns or modify old ones. Try to see what changes are called for, and anticipate how you can best respond to these needs when they come up in real life. To help you do this, we are going to use video-tape recording equipment so that you and your associates can observe what goes on and help each other see how you might have done some things differently, thus obtaining a better result. If you wish to read a general book on interviewing, *The Evaluation Interview* is a good one for technique.[1] Specific help on career interviewing may also be found in *When Man and Manager Talk*.[2]

"There are four cases. They are brief and generalized, but they provide a guide for characterization if you are portraying one of the employees.

"Those playing the role of manager should be themselves. Sometimes, however, analogies or models are helpful. We suggest that you think of yourselves as campaign managers mapping out strategy for a candidate as you conduct career-interest interviews. You're thus focusing on the strengths the employee

---

[1] R. A. Fear (New York: McGraw-Hill, 1958).
[2] Marion S. Kellogg (Houston: Gulf Publishing Company, 1969), Chap. 11.

has to offer in his anticipated jobs. Acting as a campaign manager, you take a position as the employee's advocate, trying to clarify his real values for all the world to see. It is a helping role, a consultative role. It should express a sound attitude.

"The plan for the session today is as follows. I have here a set of basic questions to be answered in a typical career-interest interview. During the first 20 minutes, read through the questions and change the wording slightly so that you keep the same sense but convert them to your own language, your own way of speaking. Then we'll divide into four groups again, each with an assigned case. Within the groups, two role-playing episodes should be video-taped, followed in each case by a critique and some resolutions for improvement. This should take about an hour. Then return to the main room, and we'll play back one or two interviews and discuss suggestions for improvement. Anyone whose tape is not played and who wishes to see himself on screen may stay afterward or make an appointment during the week to use the equipment.

"Here are the basic questions [see Exhibit 4]. Begin by making them seem as natural as possible for you."

Exhibit 4. Suggested pattern for a career interview.

Preliminary. State the reason for the discussion. Is it a general exploration? Is there another opportunity available? Has the employee been on his present assignment a long time? Did you suggest the talk, or did the man request it? Clear the air about the current situation. Is the man doing his work well? Is he not quite suited for it? Do you want him to stay, or do you feel it is wise for him to make a move? Is there no further likelihood of salary improvement or new developments?

Stage-setting opener. "As you know, we're having this discussion this morning to be sure I'm aware of your hopes for your career in general and your specific thoughts about the next couple

A Manager Training Program

Exhibit 4, cont'd.

of years. First, let me make it clear that most of us don't really know what we want to do for the rest of our lives. So I don't expect you to have a clear-cut plan. Instead, I'm interested in knowing why you chose the education program you did, how you feel about the jobs you've had so far, what seem to you to be reasonable next steps in your career, and anything else that would affect your decisions about this and future jobs. Then, if it seems a good idea, let's talk about specific changes we might make in your current assignment so that it better reflects your career interests."

1. *Starter question.* "Why don't you begin by telling me why you majored in _____ [field]?"
   Probes
   "What did you like best about the subject?"
   "What did you like least about the subject?"
   "Did your interest continue during college and afterward, or did you find that it shifted?"

2. *Basic question.* "That gives me a good picture of your academic interest. Now let's go on to consider your professional work experience. There's no need to talk about early part-time jobs, but instead, tell me about each major position you've held. And since we're thinking about the assets you bring to a career, let's discuss the special experience or knowledge or skill each job gave you. Perhaps you'd begin with your first professional job."
   Probes
   "What did you like best and least about each job?"
   "What did you do best and least well in each assignment?"
   "Under what kinds of conditions, style of manager, pressure, and constraints did you work most and least effectively?"

3. *Basic question.* "All right. That's most helpful. Now let's look into the future a bit. What sorts of jobs are you thinking about in general, and, more specifically, what would you like

Exhibit 4, cont'd.

to see happen during the next two years? Start with the long-range objectives first, if you will."
Probes
"Do you have alternate career goals?"
"What is it about the long-range goals that make them attractive?"

4. *Basic question.* "That gives me a good picture of the state of your thinking. Now, if you were to change jobs within the next couple of years, what position or positions seem like reasonable next steps?" Be prepared to offer suggestions to prime the pump on this question.
Probes
"What sorts of work changes would you like to see?"
"Why?"
"Are they consistent with your long-range ambitions?"
"What sorts of environmental changes do you desire: more or less pressure, a change in managing style, fewer or more constraints?"

5. *Qualifications analysis.* "Okay. Let's pretend we're putting together a campaign for the next job or jobs. Which occupations would make use of your strongest qualifications, and which ones would need experience or knowledge you don't have yet? Let's start with the strong points." Build a list of qualifications and gaps or points that need strengthening.

6. *Career plan.* "Now, let's get down to specifics. Suppose that two years from now you're still in this job. What changes should we make in it between now and then so that it will be more helpful to your longer-range career objectives? Also, are there some additional things you can do to put yourself in an even stronger position for the future, such as taking courses or participating in community activities?" Build a list of specific job changes feasible in the present assignment and other actions the employee can take to help himself.

Exercise (20 minutes). Participants reword the career-interview questions.

Instructions for practice cases. "Here are four typical cases on which to practice. Each group has a different one. Take a few minutes to read through the case, and then for about 10 minutes discuss the specific approach the manager should take with the person as well as some things he should avoid. Make a list of these to use as guidelines. Finally, pick two participants to play the interview, and record it on video tape. The suggested questions for interview discussion will need to be modified to fit the given situation, of course. When you have completed the first interview, discuss as a group how it went. What would you do differently if you were to go through it once more? Choose two more participants, and repeat the role playing, also video-taping it. Discuss again what should be done differently. At ——— [time], return here, and we'll look at selected interviews and discuss them as a group."

Exercise (1 hour). Each group reads and discusses its practice case and video-tapes two interviews.

Case 1: The Impatient Young Employee

Hank L. is a young salesman with the XYZ Company. He joined the firm two years ago and made it clear in his initial interviews that he wanted to get into management work very quickly.

His academic background includes a bachelor of science degree and a master's in electrical engineering from the University of Illinois and a master's in business administration from Northwestern. His sales record is good. He has met his quota each year and is well liked by customers. Hank feels he has done his tour of duty in selling and is ready for management.

Hank's boss, however, knows of no immediate openings. He will probably continue in his own job for another three or four years and thus is not about to move up, which would open an opportunity. Even if he did, there are other salesmen who have more seniority and who would probably be considered ahead of Hank.

Hank and his boss have not discussed Hank's career interests since he was hired. The meeting today is a routine one initiated by the manager to see how things stand, find out the current state of Hank's feelings, and learn what needs to be done to sustain his interest in the firm. He is a good man, and his boss doesn't want to lose him.

Assume that Hank has been told the nature of the discussion and has had sufficient time to think about what he is to say. Also assume there is an administrative guideline stating that employees will usually not be considered for advancement unless they have been on their current job for a minimum of two years.

Case 2: The Specialist with Unrealistic Goals

Tony M. is a quiet, shy individual who has achieved a high reputation as a quality control specialist. He was an apprentice by training, having joined the firm immediately after his graduation from high school. After the training period, he held a series of assignments, culminating in a job as a top toolmaker. At the age of 27, he decided there wasn't enough future in this work. He took a leave of absence and, with the help of some part-time work, managed to obtain a degree in mathematics. He then returned to the company in a quality control assignment. Over the next 15 years, he showed great creativity in advancing quality control practices. His most recent contributions have been in the statistical qual-

A Manager Training Program

ity control area, and his program implemented during the last two years has brought about a substantial cost saving. Almost all his work has been individual. There is nothing in his record to indicate that he has supervisory ability.

A week ago, however, Tony requested a career discussion with his boss. He stated that his purpose was to explore the possibility of a supervisory position. Today was set as the time for such a discussion.

Assume that Tony has not previously indicated his interest in supervisory work. Assume, too, that the manager feels the desire is unrealistic. He does see a progressively better career for Tony in the quality control area, however, and does not want to lose his talents and contribution.

Case 3: The Promotable Young Supervisor

Bob Z. has an M.B.A. from Stanford University. He joined the company on a special management training program upon receipt of his degree. Before doing his graduate work, he had had banking experience, his last assignment having been to adapt selected practices and procedures to a newly installed computer. He joined the company four years ago and has held two positions. The first was a special business planning assignment connected with the introduction of a new product. His business forecast, incidentally, has proved to come very close to reality in the interim.

Following that experience, he was named supervisor of budgets, responsible for budget compilation, expense reporting, and accounts auditing. He also directed a small manpower program for training new business administration graduates.

His manager feels that at the age of 31 he has had significant successes and is one of the high-potential employees in the firm. He feels that he is about ready for a better job. There are some choices to be made at this point: Bob could continue up the financial organization ladder, he could head in the direction of top-level staff work in the business planning area, or he could broaden his managerial base and aim at a general management slot. If Bob is interested in the last, a move in this direction would be necessary soon.

The purpose of the discussion today is to sound Bob out on his career interests and at least make a start on a decision. Assume that these possibilities have not been discussed with Bob before. Assume, too, that no specific opening exists in any of these areas right now. It's understood that there is no way of predicting which path might prove to be most rewarding or offer greatest success.

Case 4: The Employee Who Feels Left Out

The company is very aware that there is a shortage of talent in the 30 to 40 age group, and so it has conducted a big campaign to bring along the under-30 men as rapidly as possible. Training programs have been especially devised for the younger man who is short on experience. When candidate slates are drawn up, at least half of those nominated for active consideration must be 35 or less. The personnel director has a chart in his office on which the ages of appointees over the last year are recorded. Much of the wording in current instructions indicates the desire to select younger men to fill openings.

It's probably not surprising that Paul S., a competent manager of 52, feels that he is deliberately being excluded from jobs that he could (in his opinion) do very well. He has approached his boss to discuss this with him. "I feel out of it—for no reason at all that is related to my performance." The manager feels Paul is competent and would consider him for a suitable opening, but he does feel compelled to include younger men in the competition. He's in his middle 50s himself and feels he may be in the same boat, although he has been in his present position only about a year and a half.

Paul has been on his job approximately four years. He is a manager of design engineering for a line of small gadgets. In today's discussion, assume that the manager knows what Paul wants to discuss and has had time to think it over and get help (if he needs it) from the personnel director.

Review and critique of selected tapes (40 minutes). The course leader should show a video tape and ask the groups that did not work on the case to make recommendations to improve future discussions. If time permits, these can be compared with the opinions of the group to whom the case was originally referred. The same procedure should then be followed with another tape. A list of managerial career interviewing do's and don'ts should be handed out (see the accompanying box) and participants asked to add any sound new thoughts that came out of the day's discussions.

Homework assignment. Reviewing career value statements 9–13, each participant should list at least one specific action he will take to implement his beliefs and give a date when he will do or begin it.

Participants should familiarize themselves thoroughly with the basic career questions outlined in session 4 so that they can use them in the next session's interviews. Four new employees have agreed to come to session 5 to talk over their careers with participants. These interviews will be video-taped for learning purposes.

SESSION 5. Objective: To allow participants to conduct real interviews with young employees, exploring their career inter-

CAREER MANAGEMENT

Recommendations for Career Discussions

Avoid	Try
Raising false hopes about promotion.	To set realistic expectations for the discussion.
Interrupting.	To insure privacy and set aside plenty of time for reflection and continuity of thinking.
Insinuating that the only good future is up the managerial ladder.	To focus on growth in the present assignment and how it can be made more meaningful.
Evaluating the man's future for him as you see it.	To ask for his thoughts and offer information and additional suggestions regarding his future.
Criticizing the man's evaluation of his future.	To find out why he feels as he does about his future and add information.
Discouraging a stated ambition.	To discover why he has a stated ambition, and suggest alternatives, ways to learn more about it, and ways to test his interest and aptitude for it.
Evaluating a man's readiness for the career he wants.	To ask him to evaluate his competitive position.
Making commitments. You may not be able to keep them.	To limit conjecture about the future to matters within the employee's control, and make it clear when you are expressing an opinion.
Ending with analysis.	To ask the employee to translate his ideas into specific action plans.

SOURCE: Based on Marion S. Kellogg, *When Man and Manager Talk* (© 1969, Gulf Publishing Company, Houston), pp. 178, 179.

Recommendations for Career Discussions, cont'd.

Avoid	Try
Displaying a negative, uninterested attitude.	To exhibit a positive attitude; be the man's sponsor or campaign manager if he is ready.
Doing too much for the man so that his own abilities aren't tested.	To give him exposure with those who make promotion decisions, and help him prepare for this exposure.
Solving his career problems.	To provide information while letting him manage his own career.
Fixing a goal rigidly; it may be needlessly limiting.	To look at alternative goals; provide for some flexibility.
Looking too far into the future.	To focus attention on actions during the next year or two.
Recording information that the employee doesn't know about or want in the record.	To agree on what should be recorded.

ests and offering such information and counsel as seem appropriate; to pinpoint where career interviewing techniques need improvement and stimulate successful dialogs on this subject.

Introductory comments. "The session today will be almost entirely devoted to real-life career interviews with four of our relatively new employees. I have data sheets on each of them for you. We'll separate into four groups, and one interviewee will go to each group. At the end of 45 minutes, each young man will rotate to another group, and we can then compare the information drawn out by two different interviewers. When you go to your room, I suggest you take three or four minutes to familiarize yourselves with the background data on the man being interviewed. The two people who should do the interviewing in each group are [names]. These were selected because they did not have a turn at role playing at our last session. Please return here at _____ [time]."

Exercise (total 1½ hours). Interviews are taped.

Review and critique of selected tapes (1½ hours). On a random basis, select two tapes of the same interviewee. Show both without comment, and then lead a discussion on which is better and why. What might the other interviewer have done for a better result? (If the tapes are very similar, cut the second tape short and look at a second pair.) Ask each interviewee to describe any reactions he had to the way the discussion with him was conducted, the manner of the interviewer, the degree of satisfaction he received, and so on. (If desired, this could be done in writing and given to each interviewer for his personal use.) Arrange appointments for those who wish to see the remaining tapes.

Homework assignment. At the first session, it was announced that there would be about a month's interval between the fifth and sixth meetings. During this time, participants should interview at least one and preferably two of the employees who report to them and record the interviews. Each should then listen to his own interview by himself and make notes of changes he should make in the future. Each participant should bring his notes with him to the last session of this course, which will meet on _____ [date] at _____ [hour].

During this month, the actions decided upon to fulfill the career values statements should be reviewed and consolidated and a plan of action drawn up by each participant for his private use.

SESSION 6. Objective: To consolidate the learning from the previous five sessions through an exchange of actual career interviewing experiences.

A Manager Training Program

Introductory comments. "This is the wrap-up session for our career interviewing course. You have in mind at this point a set of beliefs about employees and their careers that represents the consensus of your associates. You also have your personal beliefs and action plans with which you propose to implement them. You have information at hand about how our promotion system operates, what the current business plans are, and what we believe their implications are for job opportunities in the future. You have an outline of a series of questions to help you explore career interests, and you've adapted these to your own language and style. Finally, you've practiced in role-playing situations and in real life.

"Today, I hope we can share some of the experiences you've had during the last month. What went well for you, and what went badly? What developed unexpectedly? What resolutions have you made for yourself for the future? Feel free to add anything else you believe will contribute to our learning in this difficult and delicate area."

Group discussion (up to 1½ hours). Draw out the points outlined. Do not prolong the discussion past a profitable point. Make a list of good points for managers to keep in mind.

Records (30 minutes). In the last half-hour, discuss which portion of the information obtained should be recorded and who should keep it and for how long. If your company has a form for documenting the discussions, make sure all those present know that it exists and how to use it sensibly. Exhibit 5 shows a form that might be used for this purpose. Probably as a minimum effort, the employee's expressed career interests should be recorded, together with his qualifications and specific actions he is taking to strengthen them.

Inevitably, as the sessions progress, it will become apparent that the manager's attitudes and his relationship with the em-

Exhibit 5. Format for documenting career interests and decisions.

1. Long-range career objectives:

   _____
   _____
   _____

2. Reasonable next positions or desired changes in the current position:

   _____
   _____
   _____

3. Special talents and experience that qualify the employee for the desired next position and long-range career objectives:

   _____
   _____
   _____

4. Gaps in experience, knowledge, or skill to be minimized if career objectives are to be realized:

   _____
   _____
   _____

5. Proposed action plans:

Action	Approximate time

A Manager Training Program

ployee are critical in a career discussion. These things are not taught in a five- or six-session course of the sort outlined. However, the instructor should seize opportunities as they present themselves to make this point clear and gain the participants' understanding that this is the case. Seeing themselves on video tape will further underline the point for them. Laboratory training or organization development work may well be a desirable next step to help each man sharpen his awareness of his special style, its impact on others, and changes he must make to improve his ability to establish effective relations with others.

11

A Sample Career Discussion

IN the preceding chapter, we raised the problem of the awkward discussion a manager faces when an employee tells him he is considering an outside offer. Some training was suggested to help him find the words to deal with the situation and obtain needed information. A series of questions to be adapted to special circumstances and individuals was outlined.

Because this discussion is a difficult one, some further examples might prove helpful. A specific case is therefore presented here with some sample dialog. It should be viewed merely as the starting point for a rewarding exchange, not as a definitive model. The questions used and the manager's approach are deliberately modified to show how previously presented materials may be adjusted to meet immediate requirements.

The Case of Walter A.

Walter A. is a liberal arts graduate in his early 30s. He is on the headquarters advertising staff of a retail chain and

A Sample Career Discussion

is responsible for planning campaigns for specified merchandise. He does some creative writing but primarily designs promotion programs and then works with advertising agencies to develop one or more of his ideas. He does not have final authority to approve a campaign. This is the responsibility of his boss and the head of the department involved.

His progress has been fairly rapid, although not spectacular. He is considered able, growing, and endowed with sufficient potential to make him a good candidate for his immediate manager's job should the need arise. There is no evidence, however, that this is imminent.

Walter naturally comes in contact with a large number of advertising agencies in the course of his work. He has not been seeking outside opportunities, although lately he has felt that his work has become somewhat repetitive.

One morning he receives a phone call from an acquaintance at the XYZ Creative Concern. He asks whether Walter knows anyone who would be interested in an account executive position with the firm. It seems XYZ is losing a key man to another agency and is searching for a replacement. The caller gives Walter details about the work, the salary, and other benefits the firm is prepared to offer. On impulse, since the money involved represents a substantial increase over his current salary, Walter asks, "Why don't you consider me?" The warmth with which the suggestion is greeted indicates that the caller was hoping for this response.

There follows a series of interviews with XYZ, after which Walter finds himself in a dilemma. When he is with XYZ, he sees all the advantages it has to offer. When he is back on his own job, he realizes he enjoys it, the firm he works for, and his associates very much. It becomes increasingly clear that he will be offered the job, and he concludes that, in fairness to himself and his employer, he must explore possible opportunities within his present firm. So one morning he takes the bull by the horns and asks to see his boss. When they are face to face he says, "John, I'm seriously considering an outside offer. But before I make a decision, I'd like very much to talk to you about it and explore the opportunities our company has to offer. Would you be willing to do this?"

John is shocked and distressed. He hadn't had an inkling that Walter was looking into other jobs.

"Walter, what's happened? Has something gone wrong that you're looking outside?"

Walter tells him the story of how this came about. His boss feels more or less forced to congratulate him on the offer, even though inwardly he is horrified at the thought of losing Walter and seeking a replacement. He realizes he must think through what he's going to say rather carefully. He also recognizes the need to investigate possible future jobs for Walter so that he can supply as much factual information as possible. He suggests a short delay.

"Walter, you certainly should have all the facts we're able to muster about you and your possible future in this firm. Frankly, I must look into this. If we were to get together next Tuesday, would that be soon enough for your purposes?"

Walter agrees, and the appointment is made.

The manager's first step is to examine the personnel records, official and unofficial, to learn about Walter's past contribution and any earlier expression of interests and to determine whether he is included in manpower succession lists or other rosters of high-potential people.

When he investigates, he finds that Walter is considered an excellent man though specialized in the advertising function and for this reason somewhat limited in the promotion opportunities open to him. In fact, his own job is the only one for which Walter is a prime candidate. He has simply not had any buying or selling experience, and if he were

A Sample Career Discussion

chosen for the management training program, it would probably entail a slight reduction in pay. If his performance on the program were excellent, he would recover his loss in a little over a year. But John has no idea how Walter would feel about this sort of career shift. Moreover, Walter is a key man in the advertising department, and John looks to him as his replacement. For several years now at manpower reviews, he has been in the comfortable position of knowing that he had a good man coming along, displaying all the qualities needed to run the advertising section.

John has to admit to himself, thinking about this situation, that he has not mentioned any of this to Walter. It seemed much too soon. After all, barring unforeseen events, he expected to remain in his post for another 10 or 12 years. To Walter, this might seem a very long time indeed with no (or very little) change foreseen in the scope of his present position for that period. He begins to wonder what he could do to make the interval more exciting and more developmental. "A fine time to begin thinking like this—just as the man is about to leave. We should have talked about this a year ago!"

John is right at least in his conclusion. He and Walter should have been working on the enrichment and enlargement of Walter's job right from the beginning. If it looked relatively static, they should have been discussing ways and means to vary it or provide some other experiences that would add to Walter's value. Walter, however, must share some of the responsibility for failing to do this since his is the prime interest and he is the lead figure. Away from the heat of the immediate situation, the whole career plan might have been developed more soundly.

John mulls over the problem for several days and talks it over with his own boss to be sure he agrees with the course of action John proposes. Finally, Tuesday arrives.

CAREER MANAGEMENT

The Discussion

JOHN: Walter, come on in. I can't say I've been looking forward to this discussion today. It's always difficult to be objective in a situation like this, so let me begin by saying that while I've tried to think about your opportunities objectively don't expect me to be impartial about your staying or leaving. On this, I'm just plain biased. I hope you'll stay. Your work has been excellent. You have a lot of know-how about our operation here, and frankly, I have relied on you a great deal to work with some of the department heads. Now that I've made that plain, let's really talk.

[Note that the manager begins the discussion with a completely open expression of his feelings about Walter and his work and contribution. Since there is always the possibility that this is what the employee really wants to know, it's a good way to begin when the man has requested the discussion. Even if the manager's evaluation is unfavorable, the frank appraisal of the present situation is still a good opening. It clears the air and encourages the man to be equally communicative.]

WALTER: John, thank you for that. I did want to know how you felt. It's been a while since we really sat down to talk about what I'm doing for the organization. I've felt that everything was all right. But I suppose we all look for some reassurance from time to time. [When John fails to speak but gives the impression of definite interest, Walter continues.] You know, I really wish I hadn't started all this. I like what I'm doing. I like the people I work with. I'm not quite sure why I volunteered to be a candidate. Maybe I've been feeling a little too comfortable lately. And of course, the money is quite a bit more. That probably influenced me. It still influences me, to tell the truth. I think I could do their job pretty

A Sample Career Discussion

easily, and just now, with a growing family, money is important. [He stops and looks at John very seriously.] But I don't want this discussion to be just about money. I know the salary ground rules around here. It's more important that I look at the long run—the kinds of opportunities that might exist in the future. That's where I think you can really help.

[Note that there were several pauses in Walter's comments. The manager was wise to sit quietly and wait them out. An interruption could have redirected Walter's thoughts, in which case he might not have revealed so spontaneously the basis for his interest in the prospective job. By now, it's clear what Walter expects of John and roughly what priority he has put on work content and salary. John wishes he had a better story to tell or plan to suggest. Since he hasn't, he must jump to the heart of their talk, expose the picture as he sees it, and then work with Walter to find the best solution for him.]

JOHN: I appreciate your being so frank, Walter. It shows me what attracts you to this offer and what pleases you about your present job. So let me just tell you the situation as I see it. Now, you may see more or other things than I do, so don't hesitate to speak up if this happens. I'd like us to talk this matter out to your complete satisfaction.

First of all, let's consider the advertising department. As I indicated, you are and have been a real asset to this department. You've built up good relationships with our agencies [he grins]—obviously! And you've kept some of our most demanding department heads reasonably happy with the service we've been providing them. You've contributed some excellent ideas to our sales campaigns. Although there hasn't been a great deal of opportunity for creative writing, when you have done a display ad, it's been a winner. There is just no question about it; you're well qualified for the job you're on.

Now, the problem is, what can we offer you beyond this?

We're not a very large group, and there aren't any intermediate jobs between you and me. When I filled out our succession charts last spring, I said you were the leading candidate to replace me. I still feel that way. Unfortunately, I don't see myself moving on to another job in the near future, and I'm not going to retire for 10 years! None of us can see into the future, of course. All kinds of things might happen, but I realize you can't base your plans on what might be.

WALTER [interrupting]: It's great that you think I could be your successor. That really pleases me.

JOHN: Probably I should have mentioned it to you before; but with so long a time span involved, it didn't seem appropriate. Anyway, when you came to me last week about the offer, I realized I needed to explore other possibilities. So in the last few days, I've talked to my boss and the people in the personnel department. Here's what the situation looks like to me. Your work has become specialized during the last couple of years. People think of you only in relation to advertising. When they're asked to name their back-up man, you don't come to their minds. The result is that you're not on their lists. Even the personnel office thinks of you as performing well but very much of a specialist.

WALTER: That doesn't surprise me. After all, I've never tried for other kinds of jobs or indicated an interest in anything except advertising. I don't expect people to read my mind. Even the job offered to me by XYZ is straight advertising.

JOHN: Yes. But is this the way you want it to be? You see, you and I have never sat down together and talked about what your notions are for yourself and your career, long and short range. I think we ought to do that today so we'll both be in a better position to make plans. Are you willing, or is it too late?

A Sample Career Discussion

WALTER: No. It's fine with me. I'm not sure my mind is completely made up when I think about the future, but I'm certainly willing to tell you as much as I know myself.

JOHN: Great. In that case, let's talk about your hopes for your career in general and then we'll talk about the next couple of years specifically. Incidentally, most of us don't really know what we want to do for the rest of our lives, so don't be concerned about that. Instead, suppose you begin by telling me why you chose a liberal arts program in college, how you feel about the jobs you've held so far, what seem to be reasonable next steps for you, and anything else that would affect your decision about this and future jobs. Then let's put our heads together to see if we can come up with any creative ideas that would help you right now. Begin with college. Why liberal arts?

WALTER: Well, I'll tell you. When I was in school, I hadn't any idea at all of what I wanted to do. But the courses I did best in, got the best grades in, and enjoyed most were the liberal arts courses. I liked to read and write and seemed to have a flair for short stories. I thought maybe I'd like to be a writer. But after giving novel writing a fling as an undergraduate, I realized that I was really more interested in the character development aspect of it. This led me to take psychology courses. I found I ate the stuff up.

When I got out of school, I looked for a job that would combine writing and psychology. The placement office told me of a couple of openings in ad agencies, and the work sounded good. The BLP Company offered me a job, and that's how I began. Of course, I only did routine stuff to start, but it was good experience, and I liked the work. After a while, they gave me a little more responsibility. I guess I did all right, because one day they let me try my hand at a proposal for a new account. I got it—and a promotion.

JOHN: It sounds as if you were doing very well there. What made you come to us? We were your next employer, weren't we?

WALTER: Right. Well, I'm interested in people, you see, and in the new job, everyone around me seemed very suspicious of me—as if I were out to get their accounts. There was a lot of secrecy and cover-up and, I'm sorry to say, quite a bit of throat cutting. And some of the people I thought were good friends of mine shut me out completely as soon as I got the promotion. That made me very uncomfortable. Then one day I saw a way of making life a lot simpler for all of us. The basic idea was to share some of the routine stuff. I went to the top boss with the idea. He thought it was a good one and told everybody that I'd suggested it and we were going to try it out. Boy, was I in the doghouse from that time on! You'd have thought I was trying to get people fired. Anyway, life was pretty unbearable. I saw your ad and answered it, and you know what happened from then on.

JOHN: You haven't found the same kind of competition here?

WALTER: No, far from it. People here have been friendly and helpful. Oh, they get a little uptight if their ad can't be run when they want it, but on the whole, it's a great group of people.

JOHN: I take it, then, that you put your associates and the work climate pretty high on your list of priorities for a good job.

WALTER: Yes, I do. You only have to have that kind of experience once to make you gun-shy. I wouldn't ever want to be back in that kind of situation again.

JOHN: How about XYZ? You don't feel you'd run into similar circumstances there?

WALTER: I honestly don't know. I'd completely forgotten

A Sample Career Discussion

about it until I started to talk to you today. It's certainly something to look into and consider.

JOHN: Do you think that perhaps, now you've been working longer, you could deal with such a situation more easily? Or is it the kind of thing you never learn to handle?

WALTER: Probably I'd be smarter about it now. At least I'd know what to look for. But why should anyone have to? Why not choose the right kind of environment?

JOHN: Of course. Well, that's constructive information—writing and psychology in a friendly, cooperative atmosphere, eh? Let's shift gears for a minute. Is this still the target? Looking into the future, what do you see for yourself—in the long and the short run? Start with the long run first, if you will.

WALTER: That's the hard decision, isn't it? I know I can't just go on writing motivational ads all my life. I guess I really would like to have your job. [He looks a little apologetically at John.] Now, don't get me wrong. I'm not suggesting that I'm out to displace you. It's just that your job is the only one I can see for myself.

JOHN: Fine, no problem. And I did say for the *long* run, didn't I? See how I protect myself? Now let's think about the short term. If you were to make a change within the next couple of years, what job might seem the next likely step? Let's just see if we can think of some jobs that have pretty much the same elements you like—writing and people—but would involve you in a different aspect of the business. Some of the personnel jobs—like that of the communications specialist—combine these factors. And of course, all of managing is involved with people. Have you ever thought of these?

[Notice that the manager primes the pump here, since it is clear that Walter is limiting himself to advertising department jobs. In so doing, John increases the number of possible choices.]

CAREER MANAGEMENT

WALTER: To be honest, I hadn't thought at all about personnel work. I think I'm just not geared for that. While I like people, I don't much care for the idea of writing employment ads or the daily news sheet they turn out. I think I'm more geared to marketing—trying to reach people through ads. I can't explain it very well, but to me there's a big difference.

JOHN: Yes, I think there is; and you're quite perceptive to see it. Well, how about managing? Would you like to think about running a section here in the store? You mentioned marketing. Perhaps a staff job in market research might be attractive. It's a function that will expand in the next few years. Neither would have a great deal of writing in it. How important is writing to you at this stage?

WALTER: To me, writing is an easy way to get certain results. But it isn't my main objective any more. Managing would be out, I think, because I'd really have to start back through the management training program, wouldn't I? And even if I made it, I'd have to try for an opening at the same level as the spot I'm in, so I'm not sure that I'd have gained much by the move. But the marketing work you mention does interest me. I'd never really thought about the other staff departments. And the research to find out what people want and will pay for things, as well as opening new markets or trying to enlarge the ones we've got—that'd be pretty interesting. Of course, I don't know much about it.

JOHN: Well, that gives us a place to start, doesn't it? Probably the first step should be to talk with people who are doing this kind of work to find out what they actually do all day long. Sometimes things sound glamorous, but the daily eight-to-five routine can be pretty dull. Would it be better to stop right here for the moment to give you time to investigate a little? We can get back together later today or tomorrow,

A Sample Career Discussion

whichever you prefer. If you find you're really interested, we ought to lay out a development program for you to see how it looks when we get our best ideas down on paper. Also, if you decide to look into market research, you might want to talk to some other staff groups to see if there's one that might appeal to you. What do you think? Have you time?

WALTER: Not much. But I'm going to take the time. I'll go talk to Joe right away and maybe just wander around some of those offices. Could we get together later today? I think that with this decision hanging over me, the sooner it's resolved, the better.

JOHN: Fine. Let's try for about four o'clock. But don't rush. I'll be around, and you should take all the time you need and can spare.

[The manager was wise to stop the discussion at this point. Little could have been done to develop an analysis of John's qualifications until the attractive job or jobs were better understood. Sending him off to do his own investigating is also wise. It gives him a first-hand feel for what people do and how they react to their work situation. This is almost always better than a third party's attempting to portray and interpret the job.

[At 4 P.M., Walter returns. He looks pleased with himself. He starts right off.]

WALTER: John, I'm really quite excited about what I found out. In fact, I don't know why we haven't been using their findings in our advertising campaigns much more than we have. They do a good deal of work that seems pretty interesting: sending out questionnaires, setting up consumer panels that react to new products, organizing housewife demonstration groups, and a lot of other things. Of course, I'm not familiar with some of the techniques they use, but it's pretty fascinating! One thing I have to ask right away is how salaries in that area compare with ours. There's no point in being interested if the money is no better.

JOHN: On the jobs at your organizational level, the salaries are comparable. But they offer an advantage because that's a larger department. It has some lead positions that pay more. [He names a figure.] Then there are managers for each area who report to the marketing manager. So there are more intermediate opportunities there than here.

WALTER: Right. I guessed that was probably the case. O.K., then. What would I have to do to qualify?

JOHN: All right, we're thinking along the same lines. Let's run down what you know and can do right now that would be useful for this kind of job, and then we'll look at what special action will be needed to get you ready. From what you saw today, what assets would you bring to the job?

WALTER: Hmm. I guess my college psychology courses would be a help, plus the reading I've done the last few years on motivation and buyer behavior. The advertising programs I've worked on have required me to be aware of what the social scientists are telling us about people, and even more important, I've had to apply it in our advertising. Then there's my knowledge of our store products—I think I know as much or more about their good qualities and shortcomings as anyone. I also know what people have been responding to and what they've rejected. So I'd have good common sense with which to test any market research data being studied.

JOHN: Those are two excellent pluses—particularly your experience learning what people like. You should really capitalize on that one. After all, there's always a big question about the value of polls and sample surveys and reaction panels. Having a background that prepares you to interpret the results should be a very favorable factor. The survey information might not be incorrect, but at least you'd have the foreknowledge to double-check the questionable responses. [John stops

A Sample Career Discussion

for a moment.] Can you think of other things? Would the advertising you've been preparing help directly, for instance?

WALTER [after a pause]: Perhaps not directly. But you know, one of the problems they have is to get people to reply to questionnaires. I wonder if a real promotion campaign approach to these surveys wouldn't bring a larger response. It could produce better data, or it might mean a cost reduction because we wouldn't have to send out so many questionnaires to get the same volume of response.

JOHN: It sounds like good reasoning to me. Are there some other things? [He smiles.] After all, we must put together a formidable case for you if you're going to try for the job.

[Note the manager's attitude. He has put himself squarely on the employee's side. He is in the role of campaign manager for the employee—a good model for managers to follow.]

WALTER: Yes, I think the statistical techniques we've worked out for evaluating the power of our ads could be applied to market research prediction. They do some follow-up there, but I got the distinct impression that it wasn't enough. There's another thing, too. I told you I was sorry we hadn't used their data more. Maybe there are other spots in the stores where their stuff should be used. I think that, with my knowledge of the departments, I could help find places that would be really happy to get the data. Maybe they need an advertising campaign, eh?

JOHN: Well, if they do, you're clearly the man to do it. Is there anything more you can think of?

WALTER: That's all for the moment. I'm afraid the things I don't know are more numerous!

JOHN: O.K. Then we'd better take a look to see how serious they are. The main one, I presume, is that you haven't done any market research or been formally trained for it. How much of a drawback is that likely to be?

WALTER: The last people the department has hired have

come from business schools, so I presume they've had some academic training at least.

JOHN: Specifically, what would you be missing?

WALTER: I think the main thing is knowledge of statistical techniques. I'm pretty sure I could read a good book or two on marketing and grasp the essentials. It's in mathematical skills that I'm really weak. It's been a long time since I've had any math, and it wasn't one of my best subjects. I think I'd just about have to take a night course in statistics to see if I could do it at all.

JOHN: And enjoy doing it. After all, you don't want it to be an ordeal you face every day, even if you can do it reasonably well.

WALTER: Yes, of course, you're right about that. I have to think about that a little more. It's hard to remember how I felt about math. Then there's working with the computer. I've played around with it a little here, but I can't really say I'm at home with it. In market research, they use it all the time.

JOHN: What would you have to do in order to feel comfortable with it? Would this mean another course?

WALTER: I'm sure a course would help, but I believe it would just mean some long hours working at it. The fundamentals I think I've got. I simply need lots of practice.

JOHN: So extra hours, eh?

WALTER: That's right, but I don't have to wait until I'm in the department to get going. I should be able to start right away. Now, let's see, what else? There must be something else, but I can't think of it.

JOHN: Well, if we look at advancement for you within the marketing department, there's the whole area of management. You haven't had any experience at this, have you?

WALTER: No, but at least on that one I have done a lot

A Sample Career Discussion

of reading. It's an area that intrigues me. Do you think there's something I need to do to get ready to manage?

JOHN: The number of people in the market research department wouldn't be large, so I'm not thinking of a very elaborate program. But maybe I'd ask you to do some of our budget work and perhaps to look for your successor if you should have the opportunity to make a change—things like that.

It's even more important, though, for a good manager to think about building strong day-to-day relationships with associates up and down the line. Probably your associations with people in agencies have given you good experience for this aspect of managing. It's a little different, but not so different as some people think. Just don't forget this when you're telling your story. Your competitors may have had direct management experience, so you want to be able to counteract their apparent advantage.

WALTER: You're right. And that raises another point. Where do the marketing people usually find their new talent? Do they hire from inside or outside or where?

JOHN: They always look inside, especially at the young recruits in the management training program. But in the last few years, I believe that they've had to go outside almost every time. Why not talk to someone in the personnel department to find out for sure? It is a pretty important point.

WALTER: I'll do that first thing tomorrow morning.

JOHN: Should we just see what we've got, then? On the plus side, you have up-to-date knowledge and application of psychology, especially motivation. You have excellent knowledge of the store chain, its products, what sells and doesn't, and so forth. You have some specific thoughts about special contributions you could make in research surveys, evaluation, possibly cost reduction, and perhaps new users for their information. [He looks up.] That's not bad. Now, on the negative side, you're weak in math and statistics, and you'd need some course work for these areas. You'd have to do some reading about marketing in general. You need practice in working with the computer and in some of the frequently used management skills. These we could probably work on right here. [John stops.] That's it. How does it sound to you? Have I got it all?

WALTER [slowly]: You've got it all. But—it sounds as if I only have some peripheral know-how they'd find useful; what I'm missing is the straight knowledge of the work itself. I'm going to have to do some thinking. There's a lot missing from my qualifications picture. Yet I'm sure I could do the work. It's really a tough decision. Should I risk waiting for someone to take an interest in me and give me a break, or should I accept the agency offer that's available right now?

JOHN: And of course, you have to consider what kind of future is likely to be open to you at XYZ, too. So far we've been comparing their offer with our possible future opportunities. You ought to examine what's likely to lie ahead there, too. Then I think you'd better sleep on it. Let the ideas simmer. You've got most of the facts, in my opinion. You just have to decide what they add up to for you—what risks you want to take. Let me repeat that I hope you'll stay. But you must make the decision that's right for you, now and for the future, as best you can see it.

The Manager's Contribution

For purposes of our portrayal of the situation, whether Walter decides to go or stay is immaterial. The point is that the manager contributed in a helpful way to uncovering facts

A Sample Career Discussion

that provide the basis for the decision. Let's recap some of the highlights of the approach to the discussion.

First of all, the manager made clear his own feelings on the subject as well as the facts obtainable about Walter's past record and prospects in the firm.

Next, he helped Walter examine his career to date with a few things uppermost in mind: What did he like most and least about the jobs, the environment, and the people with whom he worked in previous jobs? And what did he do best, under what kinds of conditions? These are important factors to weigh in making decisions about the future.

Once these were out on the table, John was prepared to offer suggestions that fit the picture pretty well. But he offered them as thoughts, to be explored by Walter himself. If he had taken over, Walter might always wonder whether the information given him was biased. So he sent Walter out to talk to people who could give him direct information, thus avoiding speculation.

Above all, he put himself solidly in the employee's corner—a campaign manager working with Walter to map out the best possible strategy.

He closed the discussion with a restatement of his personal feelings, since an employee often wants this but hesitates to ask for it.

In helping analyze the past, offering possible suggestions for exploration for the future, and displaying an attitude of positive interest and cooperation, the manager has done all he should do or can do unless there is a specific current opportunity to offer. Beyond this, the man must weigh the factors and reach his decision if he is to manage his own career to fit his personal values.

12

The Real World

IN the preceding chapters, we have pointed to the need for a new look at career management—one more in keeping with a participative, involved employee group and with current concepts of administration. In doing so, we have explored the limitations of the present manpower planning process and its predictive tools. We placed responsibility for career management squarely in the hands of the employee and suggested a facilitating role for employers. We pointed to ways in which the manpower planning process can and should be opened to greater influence from professional workers, and we identified actions managers and personnel specialists can and should take to assist the career advancement of special groups. Managerial training was outlined, and sample discussions were presented as illustrations. Finally, we focused on the exploratory discussion between a man and his manager as the employee access point almost universally used now in modern business.

The Real World

From all this, the impression might be created that careers advance through careful planning alone. Indeed, planning does contribute enormously to the probability of success (by the individual's definition of the term), but there are certain practical, less controllable factors in any situation that must be recognized, adapted to, and dealt with.

Career Boosts

Among the career influences frequently mentioned are luck, institutional expansion, personal chemistry, the career progress of one's boss, and sponsorship by an influential member of higher-level management. Let's look at each one of these and consider its effect and what can be done to minimize or exploit it.

Luck

Good luck is frequently named as the reason for a meteoric career rise. Its accountability is only partial. The recipient of good luck must recognize it for what it is, see the opportunity it provides, and have the talent and flexibility to respond to it and capitalize on it fully. Luck in career matters seldom resembles a lottery or even a horse race. Having made certain choices, a person cannot stand by passively awaiting the outcome. Almost invariably, there must be conscious recognition that an opportunity has presented itself, and some planned, deliberate action must be taken in order to receive its benefits. An example serves to illustrate the point.

For many years, Michael C. has had an extracurricular interest in helping those less fortunate than himself. He has been active in boys' clubs and Kiwanis and has worked many weekends and evenings tutoring high school dropouts who need school diplomas to get work. His strong drive to be of service displayed itself long before the current wave of public interest was aroused and extensive programs were developed for this purpose. On the job, Mike is an accountant working in the cost area. His company recently announced a staff department that was to be devoted solely to improving the hiring, development, and advancement of members of minority groups. When Mike heard about the new organization unit, he expressed delight that at last this problem would receive the attention it deserves. For him, that was the end of the matter. To another man in Mike's situation, the announcement might appear to be good luck working on his side. He might have seized this opportunity to bring together his job training, his experience, and his personal interest to launch a new career for himself and help his firm at the same time. Perhaps Michael C. did not want this kind of career path for himself. On the other hand, he may not have recognized the possibilities offered by the new department.

Recognizing opportunity is one essential. Having the necessary talent to exploit it is a second. The history of scientific discovery is replete with examples of chance observation of physical phenomena that permitted knowledge barriers to be broken and contributed to scientific progress. But for every man who shouts "Eureka!" countless others fail both to see the phenomenon and to interpret its usefulness. Lawrence P., for example, is a salesman with the XYZ Company. He has a reasonable though not outstanding record of success in meeting his sales quota. For months, he has been calling on customer T. in an effort to increase his use of XYZ products. Nothing has worked. When Larry is taken off the account, his successor almost immediately gets a substantial increase in orders. Luck? Not entirely. The first time the new man visited the customer, he was asked to tour the plant. During his tour, he noted a number of inefficient practices that were costing money his products would help save. When he brought the facts to the attention of customer T., he made his sale.

While luck can therefore be a legitimate contributor to success, it is far from sufficient. Each person should do at least two things if he is to capitalize on good fortune and turn it to his career advantage. First, he must take time to observe what is going on around him and reflect on its meaning for him. Second, he must develop insight regarding his favorable personal qualities and experience and the many different ways in which they might be used. Both processes can probably be expedited by a competent professional, who may be a psychologist, a vocational counselor, a management consultant, or a personnel specialist.

Expansion

Each person must define success for himself if his career is to bring him the satisfaction he deserves from his work. Probably he must redefine it at several stages of his career, since aspirations usually change as one conquers or fails to conquer hurdles and begins to understand himself and his abilities a little better.

To many people, however, success means advancement in the organization hierarchy with corresponding increases in salary. It stands to reason that a rapidly expanding concern has many more opportunities to offer than one about at its peak facing stability for the foreseeable future. The man determined to advance quickly will do well, then, not only to prepare himself adequately but to choose his employer with some care, keeping in mind the state of the art in his field, the stage of growth of the product or service he offers, and the

CAREER MANAGEMENT

plans for enlarging staff to meet expected customer needs. The aerospace industry in the late 1950s and 1960s serves as an excellent example. Salaries rose rapidly for those associated with it, and individuals assumed management status long before their classmates who had gone into other fields. The computer business during the 1960s is another instance.

Such situations do not exist without problems. In the examples cited, otherwise capable young men were sometimes given supervisory duties without adequate training and before they were ready. They were thrown in over their heads and lived in a Cinderella atmosphere. A man reporting to such a person sometimes found his personal growth stymied because his boss was unable to give him the advice, support, and guidance he needed. Inadequately prepared supervisors sometimes form hasty judgments, so some men were arbitrarily and unjustly ruled out of consideration for openings they could in fact have filled well. In addition, linked to the possibility of a great boom is almost always the specter of failure, with layoffs and halted careers.

The individual who decides to capitalize on institutional expansion in order to enlarge the number of choices and opportunities open to him needs to be extraordinarily alert to dangerous work-cycle changes and untenable situations, which he must take the initiative to sidestep. At the same time, he must not be so impatient that he cannot hold on for a reasonable period under difficult conditions. In a fast-moving and dynamic setup, people, organization structure, and priorities are likely to shift rapidly. For this reason, flexibility and a capacity to learn quickly are critically important. Perhaps most necessary is that he keep himself from being overpromoted so that he cannot perform his new job adequately. Reputations are as easily lost as gained in rapidly expanding fields. Finally, the man who chooses a boom situation needs

The Real World

enough self-confidence to face a job search without unmanageable personal stress.

In sum, then, in a rapidly expanding firm, the rate of career advancement is high; so are the risks. One should seek the level of expansion that matches not only his desires but his abilities and personal traits as well.

Personal Chemistry

Some people simply have an easier time of it than others. They are fun to deal with, pleasant to have around, attractive, and interesting to talk to. What is it about them that makes this so? When it defies concise description, we say that their chemistry is "good." In some cases, more than one person is involved. A particular manager, for instance, gets along especially well with a certain individual. Their personalities complement each other, or they have strong common interests. It may be difficult to pinpoint the exact reasons for their bond. Again, we say the chemistry between them is good.

Needless to say, good chemistry is quite an asset. Since some people have it and some do not, the important thing for sound career management is for each person to learn about himself with as much objectivity as possible. How do other people see him? What are the advantages and limitations of his personal style? What kinds of people are likely to find his style more than merely passable or acceptable? Armed with this information, he may then set about to choose the kinds of associates and situations that will give him the best break for his personal progress.[1]

An example is in order to emphasize the point. John K. is a warm, sympathetic man, a good listener, and inclined

[1] See Fred E. Fiedler, *A Theory of Leadership Effectiveness* (New York: McGraw-Hill, 1967).

toward a soft approach to associates. He finds it extremely difficult to make decisions affecting others adversely, even though the overall good of the organization sometimes dictates tough-minded actions. If John wants a leadership role, he needs to examine himself with the help of a professional counselor or perhaps in a laboratory training session.[2] In what ways are his qualities—his concern for people, his good listening habits, his warmth—especially advantageous? And what kinds of people are most likely to accept him as a leader? Perhaps a position in manager development or as a consultant or running a hospital unit might capitalize on his strengths. Moreover, developing expertise of a high order in his chosen field and selecting a staff of competent professionals who can respect his authority of knowledge and welcome his supportive approach are both likely to help advance his leadership position and make it easier for John to move ahead.

Such decisions and actions are not insurance policies for success, of course. But by choosing the circumstances in which he is likely to appear at his best, a person is managing elements that can be influenced rather than trying to compete against very tough odds. There is no one ideal set of circumstances. The person has full outlet for releasing his creativity to find a combination of environmental factors that will most enhance his personal style.

Sometimes such factors are not chosen before accepting a position but can be deliberately contrived afterward. A newly appointed manager, for instance, should look at the organization structure supporting him to be sure it is manageable for him. He should examine the way reporting

---

[2] For a good description of the laboratory method, see Edgar H. Schein and Warren G. Bennis, *Personal and Organizational Change Through Group Methods: The Laboratory Approach* (New York: John Wiley & Sons, Inc., 1965).

positions are designed, the people who report or might report to him, and even the arrangement of his office and work schedule. Often these matters can be adjusted or modified in a helpful way.

The Boss's Career Progress

"The man who gets ahead works for a man who's getting ahead." It's true that a man who moves up in the organization hierarchy tends to choose men to staff his department who have been productive for him in the past. He often gives them preference over people who, on paper at least, seem more directly experienced in the work at hand. This leads to the frequent comment, "It's all politics. It's not what you know but who you know that counts." This is discouraging for people who find themselves working for a man who doesn't seem a likely prospect for promotion. "What's all this about managing my career?" they may ask. "I don't have a chance unless I change companies."

The key to managing this situation, like any other, is to face the facts realistically and then search for the factors that can be controlled or at least influenced. That executives choose men they know they can work with effectively because they've done it before has a clear implication.[3] If a man seeks advancement, he should look carefully at the man to whom he will report when he changes his job. Either this man should be promotable so that he is not blocking others' advancement and may actually help it along, or he should have a great deal to offer in the way of know-how and experience. If the latter is the case, check with others to be sure he is able to transmit his knowledge. Some men are not aware of how much

[3] See Eugene E. Jennings, *Mobile Manager* (Ann Arbor: University of Michigan Press, 1967).

they know or are incapable of communicating it to those around them. If your prospective boss has the reputation of being a good delegator and a good developer of men, this is to your advantage. Set a time range in which to learn all you can, and consciously plan to make a change at the end of that time. This means you must be familiar with benefits arrangements so that you will not be unduly penalized if the move is to a new company. You must also familiarize yourself with the promotion system of the firm so that you will be able to use correct administrative procedures to help yourself into a new job should you wish to transfer to another part of the same organization.

What if you're one of the fortunate ones working for a man on the way up? The situation is not all favorable. First, you must determine how desirable it is for your own career to follow your boss. Some opportunities for upward movement are satisfying and rewarding and in the right direction by the person's own standards. Others may not be so advantageous. So a careful decision needs to be made on whether the opportunity offered fits into your total career picture. Then, too, it's questionable how long one man should follow another. There are dangers as well as benefits. To become too closely associated with the career of another puts you at his mercy. If he fails, you're probably in trouble, too. In another sense, it puts the leader under too great an obligation. Each time he draws a former associate into his new sphere of influence, he takes on a responsibility that narrows his own career choices. If, for example, he should receive a once-in-a-lifetime offer to join another firm, he might find himself ethically bound to his present situation just because the livelihood and careers of others are dependent on him there. No one wants this to happen. So if you're in a favored position, the follow-along career strategy may seem to work for you. But there are limits to consider. Both the leader and the follower have the responsibility of keeping their relationship from reaching a state of total dependence on each other.

Sponsorship

Closely allied with the follow-along strategy is the practice of sponsorship. Most men who have made it to the top say that they owe it at least partly to a certain individual who strongly influenced their opportunities. Such a person may have been a boss at one time, a customer, or a helpful associate. Regardless of the original relationship, he takes an interest in a capable person, displays confidence in him, and by his attitude affects the accomplishment level of his protégé to a great extent. If such a man becomes successful in his own career, he sometimes assumes a role of sponsorship. Unlike the man who puts former associates on his own staff, the sponsor simply uses his executive influence to make sure that men he knows to be capable are considered for excellent, challenging assignments whenever and wherever they open. In this way, these men become known and are further able to display their capabilities and thus develop an even wider circle of support. They are automatically considered for new, higher-level assignments as a result. Obviously, their chances for career advancement are significantly better than those of a man without a sponsor.

What does sponsorship do to the concept of career management by the individual? If you are sponsored, it's a help. If not, you have one more variable with which to deal. What can be influenced in this situation? First of all, sponsorship is usually earned. By seeking out men who have maturity and experience, we can learn a great deal if we take the time and have the patience. Sponsorship is earned by asking their counsel, not waiting for it to be offered. It is earned by responding to their advice with interest and application when it is given. And it is especially earned by living up to their confidence so that the results produced justify the extra time and effort the counselor provided. Since capitalizing on the know-how of others is one of the marks of successful men, nothing is lost and much gained by this approach. At best, you'll learn a lot and gain a sponsor. At worst, you'll still have learned quite a bit. So one thing you can do is deliberately set out to earn sponsorship.

Sometimes, unfortunately, sponsors do not stay in the good graces of top management. For one reason or another, perhaps because they lose their own sponsor, their influence diminishes or disappears. For this reason, as in the follow-on strategy, it is unwise to become too closely linked to one individual. This advice is sensible in any event, since no one man has a corner on the knowledge of the world and it would be foolish to limit the resources of your broader education and understanding in this way. So strive to learn from the experience of many others and, in so doing, increase the possibility of multiple sponsorship.

Is this currying favor? Yes. But not in the sense of compromising your own values, conforming for conforming's sake, or even just polishing the old apple. It is earning favor, and that's quite different.

Career Barriers

We've been considering certain practical factors existing in most organizations that affect career progress. One or two limitations on the person and his job deserve mention as well.

The Stereotype

Not to be overlooked in considering barriers to career advancement is the problem of stereotyping. An employee develops a strong interest and great expertise in a particular area of work at some point in his career. For a time, it is highly rewarding to be able to solve whatever problems arise in his special sphere of knowledge. Other people come to him from other organizations; he develops a reputation as an authority. While this image is forming, a stereotype is built in the minds of the managers above and around him. Whenever he comes to mind, they think of him as excellent in this area. To be sure, he is looked upon with warmth and high regard, but the close association with a single arena of accomplishment gradually begins to exclude all other kinds of work. As new jobs open, he is not even considered, because the new openings have no substantial content in his specialty. Meanwhile, for the employee, problems start to recur, and the sameness begins to weary him. He believes he is ready for another job. When he finally expresses this to his boss, he finds the barriers to a change almost insurmountable.

Employ a few simple safeguards to prevent this occurrence. Set time limits on the usefulness of certain functions, and let your boss know what you believe they are. Initiate regular career discussions to explore reasonable next positions before you're ready for a move. Put a professional counseling session in your career plans to help you rethink your values and targets. Its timing will depend on the stage of your career, but schedule it for no later than three or four years after taking a job. You don't have to move at that time; just make certain you've considered the possibility. And of course, as soon as you're aware of stagnation, make your feelings explicit either to your boss or to a specified member of the personnel office.

CAREER MANAGEMENT

The Overcritical Boss

A second barrier to career progress is the overcritical boss. Given an outstanding individual in the department, the manager's attention is constantly focused on gaps in his performance, dates missed, feelings he has trampled on, reports he has submitted late. Often overlooked are his positive contributions: creative selection of much-needed, difficult projects, streamlined solutions to problems, a varied day-to-day activity completed with so little fuss and upset that it never comes to the attention of the manager. So the appraisals sent upstairs look just like those of a run-of-the-mill man; and unless the employee assumes the initiative, his talents will remain unknown to those higher up and he will be overlooked as promotional opportunities open.

Work plans developed with your boss before you begin the work so that you agree on the level of difficulty involved can be a help in this situation. Deliberate participation in community activities, special study groups, and similar nonorganizationally structured activities can also help you to meet and be known by others outside your immediate work group. If taking these kinds of initiatives doesn't bring results, you may have to take formal steps toward a job change.

Differences in Insight

Throughout our discussions on career management, the importance of an individual's knowing himself has been stressed—what he is, what his priorities are, what he can and cannot do well, how others view him. Its absence is perhaps the most limiting of all factors. This is one of the practical realities to which you must address yourself in managing your career. There are two ways you can sharpen your awareness.

The Real World

If you lack this kind of insight, you will probably be the last to recognize it. Your best course is to seek reactions and opinions from others. Pay special attention to direct or indirect observations from your boss, your associates, and others who really care about you and your future. Sensitivity, Managerial Grid®, or, more broadly, laboratory training may be useful.[4] In addition, professional counseling by a qualified psychologist can be of considerable help.

Another practical measure is to watch for insight in the man for whom you work. If it is lacking in him, the chances of his ability to be of direct developmental help to you are small, and the probability of his moving up the ladder is low. So learn what you can from him, but plan to try for a job change after a reasonable period of learning. You may well have to take the initiative in this matter, so think through your program thoroughly and learn the ins and outs of the promotion mechanism, determining the best way to propose a change so as not to hurt anyone while still meeting your personal objectives.

An Overall Evaluation

In view of all the uncontrollables, can one really manage one's career? Yes. But it takes a thought-out objective adapted to the changing times. It takes a plan of action that works innovatively on factors in the working world open to influence and that faces up to those offering little or no choice. Even in a given situation with no options, it is usually possible to look for and identify courses of action that involve a personal decision to make a job change at a suitable point in time.

[4] See Robert R. Blake and Jane S. Mouton, *The Managerial Grid* (Houston: Gulf Publishing Company, 1964).

CAREER MANAGEMENT

Career management also requires exploration and understanding of whatever systems for advancement or promotion are available in the organization.

Career advancement means different things to different people. To some, it means climbing up the management structure. To others, it means finding work that brings satisfaction and an increased use of their talents. To still others, it means bringing about results that contribute to a better world. By whatever definition, each of us can be more effective in the future because of the better information now available, along with new tools and approaches for our use. Management can help employees and itself by opening its selection and promotion procedures to greater influence by the employee and using creative systems to facilitate and stimulate employee growth.

DATE DUE

JAN 17 '78			
OCT 29 '79			
DEC 10 '79			
MAR 27 '80			
APR 14 '80			
APR 14 '80			
MAY 21 '80			
SEP 10 '80			
MAR 20 '81			
APR 16 '81			